Vantage

Vantage

Council of Europe
Conseil de l'Europe

J. A. van Ek and J. L. M. Trim

PUBLISHED BY THE PRESS SYNDICATE OF THE UNIVERSITY OF CAMBRIDGE
The Pitt Building, Trumpington Street, Cambridge, United Kingdom

CAMBRIDGE UNIVERSITY PRESS
The Edinburgh Building, Cambridge CB2 2RU, UK
40 West 20th Street, New York, NY 10011–4211, USA
10 Stamford Road, Oakleigh, Melbourne 3166, Australia
Ruiz de Alarcón 13, 28014 Madrid, Spain
Dock House, The Waterfront, Cape Town 8001, South Africa

http://www.cambridge.org

First published 2001

Printed in the United Kingdom at the University Press, Cambridge

A catalogue record for this book is available from the British Library

Library of Congress Cataloguing in Publication data applied for

ISBN 0 521 56705 X Vantage
ISBN 0 521 56706 8 Threshold 1990
ISBN 0 521 56707 6 Waystage 1990

Table of contents

Introduction

Vantage is the third level in a series of specifications of learning objectives developed within the Council of Europe's programme for the promotion of language learning in Europe. The series is intended to offer guidance and support to the many 'partners for learning' whose co-operation is necessary to the creation of a coherent and transparent structure of provision for effective learning relevant to the needs of the learners as well as of society, which normally provides the resources. Without setting up bureaucratic mechanisms of control, it provides a series of reference points, common objectives towards the achievement of which all can work independently but in harmony – curriculum planners, examining and qualifying authorities, course designers and materials producers, teacher trainers and last but by no means least the teachers and learners through whose interaction organised learning takes place.

The series is directed towards those – probably the great majority of ordinary language learners – who want to use another language for communication with people who speak it, both for transacting the business of everyday life and for exchanging information and opinions on private life and public affairs.

It therefore sets out to define in some detail what such an objective means in practice: what users of a language are most likely to wish or need to be able to do in the communication situations in which they take part and consequently what they have to know and the skills they have to develop in order to be able to communicate effectively in those situations.

The Threshold Level may be regarded as the key element in the series, since it attempts to identify the minimal linguistic equipment which will enable a learner to deal with the more predictable situations of daily life, transactional and interactional, as an independent agent. 'Minimal' is somewhat misleading here, of course; a substantial learning effort is required, not only to cover the range of language functions and the expression of general and specific notions which constitute the building blocks, but also to gain control over them to the extent necessary to deal with the situations of use with some degree of confidence and facility. Even so, 'independence' is relative. A learner at *Threshold* level is still dependent on the goodwill of the interlocutor, especially a more experienced or native speaker.

Waystage has subsequently been developed as an early learning objective designed to provide the learner with a broad range of resources at a very elementary level so as to satisfy the most urgent requirements for linguistic survival in the most predictable situations facing a visitor.

Vantage, as the name implies, carries learners with the same needs and perspectives a stage further. What are the needs and motivations of such learners?

First, they will be aware that the principles of 'maximum exploitation of minimal means' will have given them a minimally adequate equipment to deal with a wide range of situations in daily life, and strategies to use that equipment to the best effect. However, they will realise that their ability is very limited by comparison with their ability to deal with similar situations in their native language. They can deal with straightforward situations in a straightforward way, but may feel some sense of frustration when a situation becomes more problematic and they need to understand and express ideas in a more developed way, making finer distinctions of meaning than their linguistic equipment allows. They may feel that they are unable to do themselves justice, that they are obliged to say what they *can* say rather than what they *want* to say. This feeling is common, of course, to users of a foreign language at any level, and to native speakers too when they are on unfamiliar ground. It is likely to be particularly strong, however, when a learner can cover a wide communication range, but with only a small vocabulary to deal with the vast wealth of specific notions in each area. Furthermore, whilst the exponents of language functions and general notions will have covered between them the major grammatical resources of the language, the learner at T-level will be far from having these resources under control for general purposes. They may well have figured as part of a fixed formula for expressing a particular function. Even where a structure rather than a fixed formula has been listed as the exponent of a function, the learner is not necessarily expected to be able to handle its full potential in such a way as fully to meet the criteria of accuracy, fluency and appropriateness of usage. An obvious example is the function of 'reporting (describing and narrating)' for which the primary exponent is given as 'declarative sentences'. This cannot, of course, be interpreted to mean that when narrating an event or describing a person or object, a learner after some 400 hours of initial language learning is expected to have at his or her disposal the full unbounded set of declarative sentences of indefinite complexity, using all resources brought together in the Grammatical Appendix and incorporating all the general notions set out in Chapter 6.

For these reasons, language learners who have reached *Threshold* level in a particular language and want to continue to learn are not so much called upon to do entirely new things in the language, as to meet the challenges of daily living in a more adequate and satisfying way, less restricted by the limited resources – especially perhaps in vocabulary –

which they have been able to acquire in the time available. At the same time, they will achieve a more fluent and accurate control over the communication process. Accordingly, *Vantage* level goes beyond *Threshold* level particularly in the following respects:

- the refinement of functional and general notional categories, with a consequent growth in the available inventory of exponents. In the functional area (Chapter 5), the expansion is perhaps most notable in the expression of emotions and in the conduct of discussion.

- a considerable enlargement of concrete vocabulary expressing specific notions in thematic areas set out in Chapter 7. It should be emphasised that at *Vantage* level we make no attempt to propose a defined recommended vocabulary. The needs and interests of learners are by this time far too diverse for such a proposal to be desirable or realistic. Experience takes us all in different directions and we need to talk to other people about our own situations, jobs and leisure interests. Of course, post-*Threshold* level learners will continue to share a common framework of 'universal experience' and to build up a shared vocabulary for referring to the people, creatures and objects that form the common context in which our lives are led. However, above *Threshold* level we expect learners to be more autonomous, able to take increasing responsibility for their learning and able to make more effective use of reference books and other information sources in order to develop a vocabulary appropriate to their own needs and interests. We therefore have made more use of open word classes with suggestions for an increased range of specific items which we should expect to figure in a common core.

- recognition and limited control of important register varieties. Up to *Threshold* level we have advised learners to keep to a 'neutral' register, avoiding excessive formality on the one hand and colloquial or familiar usage on the other. In moving to *Vantage* level, learners will gain more experience of the situations which call for more formal or more colloquial usage and judge when they may appropriately follow suit. Correspondingly, a number of colloquial exponents are given for those language functions in which they are more likely to occur. At the phonetic level, *Vantage* learners will be able to cope with the degree of phonetic reduction normal in informal spoken English.

- increased ability to understand and produce longer and more complex utterances. Up to *Threshold* level, it is expected that learners will mostly be participating in dialogues consisting of short turns. In many cases simple sentences or very short sequences of simple sentences will be used, the relations between them being inferred by the listener. At *Vantage* level learners will be able to follow and produce longer discourses structured by such means as the use of sentence adverbs, the anaphoric use of pronouns and generics to refer back to items already mentioned, the use of intonational prominence to distinguish given from new information, the construction of complex sentences by the embedding of subordinate clauses (though not too many!), etc. (See Chapter 8.)

• increased range and control of goal-directed conversation strategies. Up to *Threshold* level, learners are preparing to deal with the simpler, more predictable situations of daily life in a straightforward way, following the Co-operative Principle (see Chapter 4) and expecting their interlocutor to do likewise. They are able to answer the question: 'What do I say next?' by reference to the relatively fixed schemata (verbal interaction patterns) that underlie most routine transactions and exchanges of information. They are likely to have difficulty in coping with unexpected twists in conversation, or with those complications in everyday transactions that always seem to affect the customer just ahead of one in a queue! They may then use compensation strategies to enlist the aid of the interlocutor. More experienced (and sympathetic) interlocutors will most probably adjust their normal conversational behaviour to simplify the communicative task for the benefit of the less experienced foreign learner. At *Vantage* level, interaction is less constrained and both partners can act in a more flexible and natural way, following basic goal-directed conversation strategies rather than adhering as closely as possible to fixed verbal exchange patterns (see Chapter 8).

• greater sociocultural and sociolinguistic competence. Some earlier criticisms of *The Threshold Level* centred on its alleged minimalism and neglect of cultural issues. In fact, the level represented, though it attempts to set out the minimal linguistic requirements for a communicative proficiency sufficient to meet the demands of everyday living, is far from 'minimal' in the learning effort required. As for the neglect of sociocultural values, language is a socio-cultural phenomenon central to human social existence. The everyday use of any language is impregnated with the culture of the community that uses it to organise its communication. All language learning involves intercultural experience. However, in *Threshold 1990* the relation was made more explicit by the addition of a new chapter on *Sociocultural competence*, including a more detailed treatment of politeness conventions in a variety of British English often taken as a model for foreign learners. At *Threshold* level, the sociocultural is largely a matter of awareness, though learners are encouraged to act in accordance with that awareness. By *Vantage* level, the learner's grasp of interculturality will be that much deeper, so that he or she will be able to respond more flexibly to the nature of the situations of use and the interpersonal as well as the social role relations appropriate to the situation. This flexibility is of course all the more important when English is being used as a means of communication between non-native speakers. It is not to be expected that they will both conform to the same British cultural norms. Sensitivity, awareness, openness to new experience, tolerance and acceptance of sociocultural diversity are needed. To act accordingly is a sign of the increasing linguistic maturity appropriate to a *Vantage* learner (see Chapter 11).

• improved reading skills applied to a wider range of texts. Up to *Threshold* level, learners are expected only to be able to deal with written texts of a type related directly to the situations and topics set out in the extended characterisation of the global objective (Chapter 3). They are largely confined to public signs and notices, private and routine public correspondence and information in newspapers and magazines. Learners who choose to go on with language learning may be expected to have a wider range of interests, which they will wish to develop through written media – perhaps increasingly electronic as well as printed – and extended listening. As their general and more specific vocabulary expands, and their use of dictionaries, encyclopaedias and other reference materials becomes more efficient, as well as their ability to deduce word meaning from context, they will be able to select and understand more demanding texts and become increasingly able to differentiate their mode of reading, employing different strategies according to what they need to take from a particular text. This flexibility will increase their reading speed so as to cross the threshold of satisfactory 'value for effort'.

• a higher level of skill in the processes of language production and reception. It has often been remarked that the use of language by a mature adult native speaker is the most highly skilled activity anywhere to be found. We have to accept the fact that in attempting to deal with a full range of communicative tasks which arise in daily living *Threshold* learners will have problems in doing so with the very limited resources at their disposal and that they will have further problems in actually bringing those resources to bear on a particular occasion in a particular situation. Whilst learner aptitudes and abilities undoubtedly vary greatly, we cannot expect, at any level, perfect execution of the tasks, activities and processes set out in the objective, nor should we. Perfect execution would only be attainable by spending a great deal of time on overtraining at the expense of broadening experience. There is a necessary balance to be struck between extending knowledge and training performance. Thus the *Threshold* learner not only has a wider coverage than the *Waystage* learner, but also has a more consolidated and firmer grasp of the *Waystage* objectives. Similarly, in moving from *Threshold* to *Vantage*, the learner improves not only in the respects set out above, but also consolidates the *Threshold* objectives and satisfies higher performance criteria in these areas. These will include greater freedom from memory lapses, fewer mistakes and slips of the tongue, fewer blockages and hesitations, fewer false starts and incomplete sentences, a smoother utterance with better phrasing and intonation and a higher speech rate with shorter delay in response. There will be less need to use compensatory strategies. As to receptive processes, *Vantage* learners will have less difficulty in identifying words, phrases and sentences in the flow of speech, especially when phonetically reduced forms are used or when a slight foreign or non-standard accent is used. They will be better able to understand speech under noisy conditions, or with acoustic distortion in public address systems, or with interference from other sound sources. They will 'lose track' less frequently and when they do so will find it easier to break back in.

In all, *Waystage*, *Threshold* and *Vantage* now offer to all practitioners a description of the language needed to assure a learner's ability to deal effectively with the challenges presented by everyday life, presented at three levels rising from a minimal equipment to deal with the highest priority needs, through the minimum needed to deal with the full range of requirements for a visitor or temporary resident, to an enriched equipment adequate to deal effectively with the complexities of daily living. It is, of course, for the individual user to decide how to make use of this descriptive apparatus, in order to define appropriate objectives for a particular set of learners, whilst of course bearing in mind the need to co-ordinate the efforts of different providers in developing a learning/teaching system. Users can supplement the specification if some needs of the constituency are not met, or cut out elements they do not need. Items which are of marginal value to the learners envisaged can be replaced by others. The process can be articulated into more stages if a particular educational system is organised in a 'drip feed' mode, or fewer if there is a full-time intensive programme for experienced and gifted learners. With courses for non-beginners, the description can be used to specify a prior knowledge requirement as well as the objective. Modules can be derived by concentrating on some defined sub-part of the specification, as can partial competence.

This flexibility is possible because a single model has been used for the successive levels *Waystage*, *Threshold* and *Vantage*. We trust that all those concerned with planning and implementing language teaching and learning will find it useful in setting objectives which are desirable, appropriate and feasible for the particular learners towards whom they undertake responsibility.

J. A. van Ek
J. L. M. Trim
June 1996

1 The objective: levels of specificity

The objective will be formulated in three stages, or at three levels of specificity:

1 General characterisation

2 Extended characterisation

3 Specification

The *general characterisation* is meant as an overall description for rapid orientation.

The *extended characterisation* is a detailed description for all potentially interested parties, including the learners themselves.

The *specification* is a fully detailed description meant for course designers, curriculum planners, test constructors, etc.

2 The objective: general characterisation

- As visitors to, or residents in, a country where the foreign language is used for general communication purposes,

- when dealing with foreign visitors or residents in their own country, using English as a common means of communication,

- in contact with native or with non-native speakers of English in another foreign country,

- when encountering written or spoken texts in the foreign language,

the learners will be able to use the foreign language in such a way as to cope with the (principally linguistic) requirements of those situations they are likely to find themselves in, particularly:

- situations involving practical transactions in everyday life;

- situations involving personal interaction, enabling the learners to establish and maintain social contacts as well as to engage in meaningful relations in various domains of public life (e.g. business, education, welfare, entertainment);

- situations involving indirect communication, requiring the understanding of the gist and relevant details of written or spoken texts.

3 The objective: extended characterisation

1 Practical transactions

Learners are able to cope with transactional situations in everyday life. At *Vantage* level, learners are able to deal more flexibly with these situations than at *Threshold* level , when they are problematic or take an unexpected turn. With enriched language resources (especially a wider vocabulary), learners are able to express their needs and intentions more precisely, with less (though still some) need for compensatory strategies.

1.1 Contacts with officials

Note In all contacts with officials learners are able to ask for repetition, clarification and explanation, etc. of any information, questions or documents not understood, and are able to ask for the services of an interpreter and/or legal adviser in case of serious difficulty (cf. Chapter 12).

1.1.1 Immigration

Learners are able to understand and complete necessary documentation.
Learners are able to understand and answer questions concerning:

- personal identification (cf. Appendix A, section 1)

- the duration and purpose of their visit

1.1.2 Customs officers

Learners are able to understand and complete necessary documentation.
Learners are able to understand and answer questions concerning:

- whether they have dutiable items to declare

- the contents of their luggage and the value of items

- where they have come from and where they have acquired items of property

- whether items are for personal use or as gifts or for commercial use

1.1.3 Security officers

Learners are able to understand and answer questions covering:

- the contents of their hand-baggage, pockets, etc.

- whether their baggage contains specified items (e.g. electronic equipment, real or toy weapons, etc.)

- who has packed or handled their baggage

1.1.4   Police, traffic wardens, etc.
Learners are able to:

- understand and answer questions concerning:

    - personal identification

    - details of any vehicle they drive

    - details of any property lost or stolen

    - their recent actions

    - their intentions and reasons for acting

- apologise and ask for understanding of their position in case of minor infringements of regulations

- ask questions and understand the answers given regarding regulations (parking, public access to buildings, etc.)

(See also 1.11 Finding the way.)

- summon police assistance in the case of emergency (e.g. an accident, assault, robbery), giving a brief account of what has happened

1.2   Arrangements for accommodation
(See also Appendix A, section 2. 1–6.)

1.2.1   Learners are able to:

- book accommodation by letter or telephone

- enquire about the nature and availability of accommodation in tourist information offices or travel agents, or on arrival at a hotel, guest house, camp site, etc.

- complete registration forms

- complain and secure rectification of poor service, malfunctioning equipment, etc.

- complete departure procedures, query bills, etc.

1.2.2   Accommodation for temporary residents
Learners are able to:

- enquire, in writing or speech, about accommodation to rent, e.g.:

    - the number, type and size of rooms

    - the cost (per week, month or year) and terms of letting

- the charges for services and amenities provided (e.g. local taxes, gas, water, electricity, etc., furniture and household equipment)

- the arrangements for repairs and maintenance

• make and confirm inventories of contents and their condition

• make arrangements for and supervise household removal

• make arrangements for services, repairs and maintenance as required

• make oral and written complaints to landlord

1.3 Arrangements for meals
(See also Appendix A, section 10.)

1.3.1 Eating out
Learners are able to:

• read and understand advertisements for restaurants, menus, etc.

• discuss the relative merits of accommodation, food, prices, waiting time, etc.

• ask for a (particular) table

• order food and drink

• ask and understand answers to questions on the nature and preparation of dishes

• ask for bill, enquire whether service and tax are included

• query and complain of slow service, poor food, overcharging, etc.

1.3.2 Eating at home
Learners are able to:

• read instructions for safety and use of kitchen equipment

• read content information on packets, tins, etc. and instructions regarding food preparation

• follow recipes and oral instructions

1.4 Shopping: buying consumer goods
Learners are able to:

• read advertisements in newspapers, magazines, etc. for shops and consumer goods

• read explanatory documentation (brochures, package labelling, etc.) on the nature, use and conditions of sale of goods

• read signposting in supermarkets, departmental stores, etc., as well as details printed on tins, packets, bottles, etc. on display concerning their contents and use

- ask whether goods are available and where they are to be found

- discuss the nature and relative merits of particular choices of goods

- negotiate prices and understand conditions of sale

- make payments and if necessary query prices, addition of bills, etc.

- return faulty, inappropriate or unwanted goods and negotiate replacement, refund, etc.

1.5 Using public transport
Learners are able to:

- read published information (e.g. timetables, types and conditions of sale of tickets)

- enquire as to cost, times, routes of journeys

- discuss relative merits of different means of transport and companies (e.g. duration, cost, conditions of travel)

- order, query and pay for tickets (e.g. destination, class of travel, single or return, route, dates), reserve seats, etc.

- enquire as to location of gates/bays/platforms/quays, etc. of planes, buses, trains, ships, etc.

- register luggage for despatch, use left luggage facilities, report loss of or damage to luggage and property.

- enquire about the existence of special rates, etc. and their terms and conditions

1.6 Using private transport (car)
Learners are able to:

- read, query and complete documentation for car sale or hire

- read mandatory and advisory official road signs

- obtain petrol, oil, water, air and services at service stations

- report and secure repair of mechanical faults and breakdowns

- exchange necessary car and insurance details in case of accident

(See also 1.1.4, Contacts with police, traffic wardens, etc. and 1.11, Finding the way.)

1.7 Using information services
Learners are able to:

- make personal and telephone enquiries

- read informational brochures, leaflets, etc.

- consult reference works in public libraries, etc., such as directories, manuals, guides, etc.

1.8 Visiting public places (museums, theatres, stadiums, discos, etc.)

Learners are able to:

- read published guides to tourist attractions, entertainment guides in newspapers and magazines, brochures of particular institutions, posters, handbills, etc.

- enquire about opening times, prices of admission, performance times, position and nature of seats

- book tickets in advance, or purchase at time of admission

- enquire about facilities and amenities (toilets, refreshments, programmes, etc.)

- read poster displays, notices, descriptive captions, etc. in museums, exhibitions, etc., designed for the information of the general public

1.9 Using public services
1.9.1 Post office

Learners are able to:

- read simple published regulations, counter signs, etc. for specific information

- enquire about postage rates, etc. (e.g. first and second class, letters, postcards, destination categories, registered and express post, parcels, telegrams and fax facilities)

- purchase stamps, postal and money orders

- complete customs declarations, registration forms, etc.

(for temporary residents)

- use post office facilities for licences, etc.

1.9.2 Telephone

Learners are able to:

- read instructions on use of telephone

- consult telephone directories (including yellow pages)

- use telephone directory enquiries

(See also language functions 5.20.)

1.9.3 Bank

Learners are able to:

- read public notices (especially service tills, currency regulations and exchange rates)
- enquire about exchange rates for notes/travellers' cheques and commission charges, and query amounts if in doubt
- understand and follow instructions on automatic cash-distributing or money-changing machines

(for temporary residents)

- enquire about, set up and use bank accounts

1.9.4 Medical services
Learners are able to:

- read notices (e.g. consultation hours, specialisms, signposting of hospital departments, instructions to patients)
- ask for a hospital or general practitioner appointment (by telephone)
- explain nature of complaint and answer questions on place and nature of ache or pain and other symptoms
- understand instructions for treatment at the time and subsequently
- obtain medication from pharmacist and understand information and instructions for use printed on pharmaceutical products and accompanying leaflets

1.10 Educational services (for temporary residents)
1.10.1 As students
Learners are able to:

- read brochures (e.g. of ARELS, British Council and particular teaching institutions and language schools) and follow admission procedures
- understand and use target language as medium of instruction and as language of social interaction in English language classes and among learners during breaks, at mealtimes, etc.
- report and discuss problems relating to learning, teaching, study facilities, social activities, accommodation, canteen meals, finance, school administration, etc.
- discuss and enter for examinations
- read examination regulations, rubrics and questions and respond appropriately

1.10.2 As parents
Learners are able to:

- enquire about arrangements/options for the public/private

education of their children (e.g. types of school, entry requirements, costs, dates of terms, equipment required)

- make day-to-day arrangements for school attendance
- read notes and reports on children's progress
- attend parent/teacher meetings and discuss children's progress

1.11 Finding the way
Learners are able to:

- ask for and understand oral instructions on finding the way in a particular locality
- read maps (road maps, train, tube and bus networks, and other direction signs and instructions)
- enquire from officials, service station staff or members of the public how to reach certain destinations, where a particular road or railway line leads to, the destination of a bus or train, etc.
- give similar information to others

1.12 Communicating at work
1.12.1 As temporary residents
Learners are able to:

- seek work permits as required
- enquire (e.g. from employment agencies) about the nature, availability and conditions of employment (e.g. job description, pay, hours of work, free time and holidays, length of notice)
- read employment advertisements
- write letters of application and attend interviews giving written or spoken information about own personal data, qualifications and experience and answer questions about them
- understand and follow joining procedures
- understand and ask questions concerning the tasks to be performed on starting work
- understand health, safety and security regulations and instructions
- report an accident and make an insurance claim
- make use of welfare facilities
- communicate appropriately with superiors, colleagues and subordinates
- participate in the social life of the enterprise or institution (e.g. canteen, sports and social clubs, etc.)

1.12.2 **As members of the host community**
Learners are able to

- assist an English-speaking (native or non-native) visitor or resident with the tasks listed above

1.13   Private hospitality
(See also Language functions, socialising.)

1.13.1 **As hosts**
Learners are able to:

- issue an invitation, spoken or written

- greet and introduce guests

- explain about features of domestic arrangements

- follow social routines and exercise socialising functions

- exchange information and opinions on personal and social themes

- receive or exchange souvenirs or small gifts

- say goodbye to guests and react appropriately to expressions of appreciation

1.13.2 **As guests**
Learners are able to:

- reply appropriately to accept or decline spoken and written invitations

- exchange greetings with host and other guests, known or newly met, whether introduced or not

- follow social routines and exercise socialising functions

- exchange information and opinions on personal and social themes

- offer flowers or other small gifts

- express appreciation of hospitality given

- take leave, making or confirming travel arrangements as required

2   Social interaction

Learners are able to converse with other native and non-native speakers on a variety of topics relating to their everyday lives, experiences, opinions, etc. At *Vantage* level this ability extends beyond the relatively brief conversational turns appropriate to *Threshold* level to the reception and production of longer sequences of coherent discourse and to argumentation.

Learners are able to:

- exchange information
- express, and understand the expression of, opinions, views, attitudes, emotions, wishes
- agree upon and carry out co-operative actions

The above in relation to topics of their own choosing, such as:

- personal life and circumstances
- living conditions and household activities
- trade, profession, occupation
- education
- free-time activities
- travelling, regions, places, sights
- consumer goods, shopping, prices
- eating and drinking
- social relations, religious beliefs and practices
- politics, current events, economic, social and cultural issues
- weather
- languages, language learning, language problems

For details, see Chapter 7 and Appendix A.

3   Dealing with texts

The learner can understand written and spoken texts which are relevant to the situations listed in Section 1 above or to the topics in Section 2 above and which have the following characteristics:

- they have a reasonably clear structure, both conceptually and formally
- the information contained in them is offered explicitly, or requires only a moderate amount of interpretation and inferencing
- their understanding does not require close familiarity with a particular foreign culture
- they are produced in an accessible form:
  - written texts are clearly hand written or printed and, when appropriate, provided with titles, paragraphing, illustrations, etc.
  - spoken texts are produced with little acoustic distortion, noise or

interference using standard forms and pronunciation, or a reasonably close approximation, and at a speech rate which is within normal range

At *Vantage* level the learner is able to deal appropriately with different text types according to his or her needs and intentions with respect to them, in some cases extracting gist or relevant detail, in others reading or listening with close attention to detail and using reference aids where necessary (and possible). *Vantage* learners will be able to deal to a greater extent with unstated implications, euphemisms, irony and metaphoric usage, as well as with unfamiliar cultural elements, given that the text provides adequate clues to their understanding and interpretation. A *Vantage* learner can deal with handwriting which is clearly legible, and with typewritten and printed texts containing some errors and less clear typography (faded, smudged or using a wide variety of fonts). Speech can be understood at normal conversational speed (c. 150 words per minute) with the normal degree of phonetic reduction and using the regional or national accents in current use by educated speakers of Standard English of a particular regional or national provenance (but free from dialectal features of grammar and lexicon). A *Vantage* learner will also be able to understand speech in a somewhat noisier environment or with slight acoustic distortion, especially when the message is familiar or expected. He or she is capable of recognising the phonetic form of unfamiliar words and storing them in memory so as to enquire later as to their meaning and spelling.

4   Social conventions and rituals

In connection with Sections 1 and 2 above the learner is sensitive to, and able to act appropriately with respect to relevant social conventions, e.g.

- *non-linguistic:* physical contact (hand-shaking, kissing, touching, etc.), significant roles of gesture and mime, etc.

- *linguistic:* verbal ways of drawing attention, ways of addressing, choosing degree of formality/informality, turn taking, contact ending, etc. as well as normal conventions of politeness. (See Chapter 11.)

The learner is also familiar with relevant social rituals, e.g.

- visiting rituals (appropriate time for arriving, present giving, acceptable conversation topics, etc.)

- eating and drinking rituals

- acceptance and refusal rituals

5   Interpretation strategies

In connection with Section 3 above the learner can use appropriate interpretation strategies both as a reader and as a listener, e.g.

- distinguishing main points and secondary points

- distinguishing fact from comment

- identifying relevant information. This may involve determining the audience for whom the text was produced and the attitudes and communicative intentions of the author, as well as drawing inferences from what is explicit in the text

- making use of clues such as titles, illustrations, typographical devices (e.g. bolding, italicising, underlining, paragraphing), and, in oral texts, such discourse markers as the placing of emphasis, structurally relevant pauses, tone of voice, etc.

6   Sociocultural considerations

The learner has some familiarity with characteristic features of the culture of the major countries where English is used as native language (especially those in the British Isles), particularly those affecting:

- everyday life

- living conditions

- interpersonal relations

- major values and attitudes

At *Vantage* level learners are aware of the dangers of misunderstandings arising from differences of culture and the associated conventions and rituals (see 4 above). In Europe they are aware of the principal sociocultural differences between their own community and those of native speakers of English and can distinguish stereotypes from reality. When dealing with other (especially non-native) speakers of English whose cultural background is unfamiliar, they are alert to evidence of cultural difference, able and willing to make allowances and react sensitively as well as to exchange information with the partner about their respective cultural backgrounds, expectations and behaviour.

7   Compensation strategies

The learner can use techniques and strategies for coping with demands of situations which go beyond his or her non-linguistic and/or linguistic repertoire, e.g.

- engaging a communication partner's co-operation in filling a gap in one's know-how

- appealing to tolerance of a foreigner's linguistic limitations, etc.

- strategies for 'getting one's meaning across' in spite of linguistic inadequacies

- strategies for deriving meaning from texts in spite of the occurrence of unknown elements

- strategies for enlisting the communication partner's help in solving communication problems

- using appropriate aids such as monolingual and bilingual dictionaries, thesauruses, grammars, encyclopaedias, electronic aids and other reference materials.

4 The objective: components of the specification

Vantage, like its predecessors *Threshold* and *Waystage*, is conceived as a contribution to improved communication, particularly among Europeans of all backgrounds. A communicative approach aims to enable the learners to use a foreign language for their own purposes. What these purposes are, depends on the personality, the circumstances, the needs and interests of the learners themselves. They are never fully predictable, but, starting from a particular target group, however heterogeneous it may be, we can make an attempt to identify those things that all of them are at least very likely to need or wish to be able to do in the foreign language. In order to do this in any useful way we have to try to determine in what situations they are most likely to use the foreign language, what roles they will play in these situations, and what matters they are most likely to have to be able to deal with in the foreign language. Determining all this – especially if we want to arrive at a fairly detailed description – is, in a way, a matter of guesswork. However, we can make at least better educated guesses if we make use of our collective experience, our knowledge of the world, and of whatever amount of consensus would appear to have been – explicitly or implicitly – achieved. In fact, the information on this that is available by now is by no means negligible. It may be found in numerous studies that have appeared since *The Threshold Level* was originally published, and it is to be found in the choices made in those course materials with a communicative orientation that have been produced in the last fifteen years or so. By and large, the assumptions made in the original *Threshold Level* would seem to have been widely upheld, so that the basis upon which the present specifications are built is a more solid one than for that earlier version. Yet, it should be constantly borne in mind that these assumptions are made with regard to what the members of the very large target group defined in Chapter 2 are supposed to have in common and that the undoubtedly considerable individual differences among these members are deliberately left unspecified. This is just another way of saying that *Vantage* is a general objective only, and, moreover, one that is never to be regarded as fixed and closed but as something to be used flexibly and creatively.

In the preceding *general characterisation* and particularly in the *extended characterisation* we described the *Vantage* objective. The question is now how this may be most usefully specified, how it may be broken down into a coherent set of elements that may serve the purposes of those for whom the specification is meant.

Our starting-point remains the situations in which the learners are most likely to find themselves. Each situation will make its own demands on their communicative resources. At the same time, these demands have a lot in common, something which requires what we may regard as general communicative ability. An economical description, then, of what the learners need to be able to do, will specify the components of this general communicative ability plus, for each situation envisaged, the specific ability required to function adequately in it. The general ability, the ability required in most communication situations, will be the subject of by far the greater part of our specification. In fact, there will be only one component that is directly concerned with specific situation-related ability, and – as it is to be expected – this will largely be a matter of concrete vocabulary items. A communicative approach does not consider *knowledge* of the language – however desirable this may be – as an end in itself. Its goal is the ability to *use* language, to *do* with language the kind of things one needs or wants to do with it.

The starting-point of the specification of our objective, then, is a list of the kind of things people may *do* by means of language. These are things such as describing, enquiring, denying, thanking, apologising, expressing feelings, etc. We refer to these things as 'language functions' and we say that in saying, for instance, '*I'm sorry*' people fulfil the language function of apologising or of expressing regret. The first component of our specification is a list of those language functions that the members of our target group are likely to need to be able to fulfil. The categories and exponents presented in Chapter 5 are modestly increased from *Threshold*, which already affords a wide range.

Language functions are not fulfilled in a void, with regard to nothing. If we say '*I'm sorry*', we apologise for or express regret about *something*, even though we may not mention this explicitly because it is sufficiently clear from the context in which the utterance is produced. If, however, we were to say '*I'm sorry for being late*', we explicitly refer to a particular concept, the concept of 'lateness'. The concepts that we may refer to while fulfilling language functions will be indicated here as 'notions'. Among the notions we distinguish 'general notions' and 'specific notions'. General notions are such as may be expressed in almost any situation and specific notions are those which are likely to be expressed typically in particular siuations only. In most situations the need may arise to refer to time, to place, to quantity or quality, to express relations between entities, etc. The notions involved in doing so will be listed in our second component (Chapter 6) as 'general notions'. A notion such as 'timetable', on the other hand, is likely to be expressed only in a situation of people dealing with 'travelling'; the notion of 'potatoes' is most likely to be expressed in connection with 'eating' or with 'agriculture'. Such situation-related or topic-related notions will be listed in our third component, 'specific notions'. In this third component we shall also give general indications as to what people will be supposed to be able to do in each of the situations or with regard to each topic included here. Such indications facilitate and justify the selection of those notions which may be thought particularly relevant to the members of the target group.

At *Vantage* level, learners can be expected to have progressed beyond *Threshold* level in a number of ways. They will have an enriched vocabulary for dealing with the concrete details of the situations of use identified in *Threshold*. Where these involve themes and tasks of concern to all learners, we may consider that the 'common core' of language learning has been consolidated and extended. However, learners will undoubtedly wish to discuss their special leisure, cultural and professional interests in greater depth with other people who share them. We cannot specify the vocabulary needed for these purposes as a general learning objective. We can only identify the categories within which learners will develop a vocabulary unique to themselves as a result of their experience of life. Topic-related tasks and lexicon are discussed in Chapter 7 and exemplified in Appendix A.

By specifying language functions, general notions and specific notions in relation to themes and tasks, we identify the basic elements of communication. The elements are usually combined. Most sentences contain all three. Thus *'I'm sorry to be late for dinner'* combines the function of 'apology' with the general notion of 'lateness' and the specific notion of 'dinner'. Clearly, such combinations are very large in number, so that the expressive power, even of simple sentences, is very great. At *Waystage* level, the contribution of a simple sentence to a conversational exchange, or perhaps a short sequence of simple sentences, is a suitable objective. Chapter 8 demonstrates that, in spoken interaction, such a sequence can be very effective. The greater resources available to *Threshold* learners enable them to express the interrelation of ideas and thoughts in a more compact and explicit way and to follow through the schemata of predictable verbal exchanges. In the absence of such schemata they will probably find it advisable to express themselves straightforwardly in accordance with the 'co-operative principle', that is to say that they will do their best to speak simply, sincerely, relevantly and clearly, making their contribution such as is required, at the stage at which it occurs, by the accepted purpose or direction of the interaction in which they are engaged. By *Vantage* level, greater control over greater linguistic resources enables the learner to rise above stereotypical schemata and to make more varied, flexible and effective use of principles of discourse structure and verbal exchange. These matters are treated in Chapter 8.

At *Vantage* level, it is expected that the spoken and written texts with which learners will wish to deal will be longer, richer and more various than was the case at *Threshold* level. We have to distinguish here between the use of texts as language teaching and learning materials, means to the achievement of a different communicative objective (e.g. prose passages in textbooks, or extracts from contemporary novels as examples of conversation structures and strategies) and the text types which learners wish to read authentically as an objective in its own right. It is of course the latter which are the concern of Chapter 9.

Similarly, Chapter 10 is not concerned with the written tasks involved in language courses and examinations, but with the place of authentic writing in the daily lives of those who have reached *Vantage* level. Since *Vantage* does not aim to cover the professional domain, the role of writing specified as a common objective remains relatively restricted. Letters of all kinds and informal notes are primarily envisaged. Of course, some learners – probably a minority – will make more use of the written medium or less as the case may be. As time passes, the use of information technology may well change the role and the nature of writing in daily life. However, we do not consider that this point has yet been reached.

Communicative interaction within a particular language community is largely governed (though rarely determined) by the social conventions observed in that community regarding 'who says what to whom, how, when and where' (cf. D. Hymes, 1971, 'On communicative competence' reprinted in J. B. Pride and J. Holmes, 1972, *Sociolinguistics*, Harmondsworth: Penguin.) Even at *Threshold* level, where the learner's use of language seems most appropriately neutral in register and straightforward in character, an awareness of the sociocultural context and its effect upon linguistic and other behaviour is essential if intercultural misunderstandings are to be minimised. At *Vantage* level the learner will be more familiar with the conventions and able to act more flexibly with regard to formal and colloquial registers and the politeness conventions of a host community, more alert to cultural differences and skill in coping with them. These issues are dealt with in Chapter 11.

In many real-life situations the learner's language resources will fall short of what the situation requires. Successful communication will then depend on the learner's ability to find ways of overcoming the obstacle by employing compensation strategies. This ability is particularly important in earlier stages of learning, when the resources available are very modest. However, the problem still arises at *Vantage* level. Although the resources are greater and better controlled, the expectations of the learner are also raised. Indeed, mature adult native speakers, faced with 'the intolerable wrestle with words and meanings', not infrequently find their 'shabby equipment' inadequate for the purpose! (Quotations from *Four Quartets: East Coker II and V*, in T. S. Eliot, 1969, *Complete Plays and Poems*, London: Faber and Faber.) The compensation strategies which they have acquired by *Threshold* level, dealt with in Chapter 12, remain useful and with increasing experience may more readily be brought to bear.

In the transition from *Threshold* to *Vantage* learners will necessarily diverge in their language development in accordance with the diversity of their interests and experience. The individualised learning which is involved necessarily requires each learner to take charge of his or her own learning. Responsibility will be progressively transferred from teacher to learner, who must be technically competent to undertake it. The knowledge, skills and attitudes which enable learners to function autonomously are therefore, in our view, not to be regarded as merely spin-off from the process of language learning, but as objectives to be purposively pursued. Chapter 13 is devoted to their specification.

Finally, the *Vantage* learner has progressed beyond *Threshold* not merely in the increased content of learning but perhaps even more in the degree of skill with which the language resources are deployed. That is to say that qualitative development is at least as important as quantitative development. The 'threshold' concept is based on the maximal use of minimal resources. 'Minimal' has a qualitative aspect as well as quantitative one. At *Threshold* level the criterion is the success of communication. The learner who is not content with having reached a threshold of communication adequate to deal with the situations of daily life may not so much wish to deal with more situations as to improve the quality of performance, to reduce the gap between the way those situations can be dealt with in one's mother tongue and in a foreign language, to do better justice to one's feelings and ideas. Though we do not feel able to quantify quality in the same way that content may be specified, we discuss in Chapter 14 the skill parameters of accuracy, appropriacy and fluency as criteria.

Following a discussion in Chapter 15 of some valuable 'by-products' of language learning which we have not regarded as integral components of our objective, appendices are devoted, first, to suggested lexical exponents of specific notions which may be needed to deal with the themes set out in Chapter 7 (Appendix A), secondly, to grammar at *Vantage* level (Appendix B), and, thirdly, to pronunciation and intonation at *Vantage* level (Appendix C).

Other appendices of *Threshold 1990* have not been reproduced in *Vantage*. Since *Vantage* subsumes *Threshold* in the same way that *Threshold* subsumes *Waystage*, they are of course valid at the higher level. However, since they are available to *Vantage* users in the earlier publication no useful purpose is served by simply replicating them here. In order to preclude the erroneous impression that we are advocating a defined vocabulary for *Vantage* learners we refrain from including an overall index of the words to be found in the exponents of the *Vantage* categories set out in Chapters 5 and 6 and in Appendix A of the present document. Nor, in the light of experience, have we found it necessary to include a subject index.

5   Language functions

Introduction

The *Vantage* learner, like the *Threshold* learner, is one who wishes to use a language (in our case English) to transact the business of daily living and enter into relations with the other speakers of that language in the situations which bring them together. For this reason there is no fundamental difference between language functions at the two levels. *Threshold* already covers a very wide range, though it does so with highly restricted means. To a large extent, the *Vantage* learner will cover the same broad range. Thus both *Threshold* and *Vantage* learners will need to assert facts, describe people and things and narrate events (cf. Section 1.2). However, the range of declarative sentences which a *Vantage* learner will be able to use will be much greater. That is, however, largely a matter of the means for expressing general and specific notions rather than of the function itself. (It should not be forgotten, of course, that the material for the exponence of functions is also available – often by no more than a change of person or tense – for referring to them in the course of a narrative or description. 'I am in a bad mood' expresses ill-humour. 'I was in a bad mood' or 'he is in a bad mood' reports rather than expresses that state of mind.)

Accordingly, we have seen no reason to change the broad categories in which language functions are classified. Beyond some minor reorganisation – seeking and granting permission have, for instance, been treated together with requests rather than under modality, while self-correction and hesitation fillers have been moved from Section 5 to 6 – the principal developments in a learner's expected ability to express functions are:

- *a more sensitive sub-categorisation of functions*
  particularly those in which a personal reaction, intellectual or emotional, is called for. Thus the single *Threshold* level category 1.4 'asking for confirmation' is amplified in *Vantage* level 1.4 to six, distinguishing between questions which are neutral and those which expect or demand confirmation of a statement or cast doubt upon it.

- *a greater variety of exponents*
  Thus the two possibilities for denial in *Threshold* level 2.4 are increased to nine in *Vantage* level 2.1.6 in addition to the four introduced for 'strong disagreement' (2.1.2.1). These allow a learner to distinguish between more or less formal responses and to express shades of feeling as opposed to the neutrality which characterises *Threshold* level. This applies particularly to 2.5, expressions of

emotion, expanded from 22 to 37 categories and sub-categories involving 194 rather than 102 exponents. This greater richness of resources for affective self-expression (and of course for recognising the emotions of others) involves a large number of fixed idiomatic expressions, or fixed frames for structural and lexical variables. As Palmer has said, spoken English is particularly rich in such expressions, which a foreign learner cannot simply invent from general grammatical and lexical resources for the expression of general and specific notions.

Suasion, deciding on and managing courses of action, is also expanded to give the *Vantage* learner greater flexibility and control over the management of personal relations in a wider variety of situations. At *Threshold* level, 'requesting someone to do something' is a single category for which seven exponents are offered. At *Vantage* level, eight sub-categories are distinguished, with 26 exponents. In declining offers and invitations, firm refusals are distinguished from demurring or weak refusals, which invite the renewal of the offer.

On the other hand, resources for socialising and communication repair are only marginally increased; both are priority requirements which are already well-developed by the time *Threshold* level is reached and further progress is likely to be in the fluency and naturalness with which the resources are used.

• *more developed realisation of structural variables*
Threshold (and even more *Waystage*) follows the fundamental principle of 'maximal use of minimal means'. By *Vantage*, learners will have increased the linguistic means at their disposal and will be able to organise them with greater facility.

Language functions for *Vantage* and recommended exponents with examples

Conventions
In the following section, the functional categories are numbered and shown in bold print, e.g. **1.1 identifying and specifying**. Exponents are shown below the category, each preceded by a bullet. Actual words to be used are given in bold e.g. **him/her/them**. Structural variables are given in medium sans serif, using abbreviations where appropriate. The most common abbreviations used are:

NP = noun phrase
VP = verb phrase
VP(inf) = verb phrase with verb in the infinitive
VP(gerund) = verb phrase with verb in gerund

adj = adjective
adv = adverb
be = an appropriate form of the verb *to be*

Optional elements are placed in brackets. Thus, **this (one)** means: either *this* or *this one*.

Alternative elements are placed between slashes. Thus **these/those** means either *these* or *those*.

Wherever the exponent of a functional category contains a structural variable, an example is given immediately below it. It should be emphasised that these are *examples* of exponents, not the exponents themselves. Thus category **1.1 identifying and specifying** has as an exponent Pronoun/NP + **be** + NP, meaning that either a pronoun (I/you/he/she/it/we/they/this/that/these/those) or another noun phrase is followed by the appropriate form of the verb *to be* and then a further noun phrase. In the two examples given, This is selected as a pronoun and The animals over there as an initial noun phrase. These are followed respectively by is and are as appropriate forms of the verb *to be* and the bedroom or my dogs are examples of the second NP. Examples are given in sans serif text, except sometimes where a written text is specifically indicated and italics or other special devices are used (5.6.2, 5.6.3 and 5.21).

1 Imparting and seeking information

1.1 identifying and specifying
- **this (one)/that (one)/ these/those; him/her/them** (with indicating gesture, e.g. pointing, nodding)
- **the (adj) one + adjunct phrase/relative clause**
  the small one with the blue buttons
- **It's me you/him her/us/them/NP**
  It's the postman.
- **Pronoun/NP + be + NP**
  This is the bedroom.
  The animals over there are my dogs.

1.2 stating and reporting (describing, narrating)
- **(sequences of) declarative sentences**
  The train has left.
- **NP + say, think + complement clause**
  He says the shop is shut.
- **NP + ask, wonder + indirect question**
  He asked where they were going.
- **there + be + NP + adjunct**
  There is a bank on the corner.
  There is a cow in our garden eating the plants.

1.3 correcting
- **As 1.1 and 1.2, with contrastive stress**
  This is the bedroom.
  The train *has* left.

1.3.1 correcting a positive statement
  (e.g. Valetta is in Italy.)
- **No + tag, with falling-rising intonation**
  'No, it ˇisn't.
- **negative sentence (fall-rise) + corrected positive sentence (falling)**
  Va·letta 'isn't in ˇItaly. It's in Malta.

1.3.2 correcting a negative statement
(e.g. We didn't go to London.)
- **Yes** + tag question (with falling-rising intonation)
  'Yes, you ˅did.
- positive statement (with fall-rise on auxiliary verb)
  You ˅did go to ·London.

1.4 **asking**

1.4.1 asking for confirmation or denial
- interrogative sentences (with low rising intonation), positive or negative
  'Did you ˏsee him?
  'Didn't you ˏsee him?
- **Please (can) you tell me whether...**
  Please tell me whether you saw him.

1.4.2 demanding confirmation or denial
- interrogative sentences with low falling intonation (+ **Yes or no**)
  'Did you ˎsee him, 'yes or ˎno?

1.4.3 expecting confirmation
- positive statement (falling) + negative tag (rising)
  You ˋsaw him, ˏdidn't you?
- negative statement (falling) + positive tag (rising)
  You 'didn't ˋsee him, ˏdid you?

1.4.4 demanding confirmation
- positive statement (falling) + negative tag (falling)
  You ˎsaw him, ˎdidn't you?
- negative statement (falling) + positive tag (falling)
  You 'didn't ˎsee him, ˎdid you?

1.4.5 querying a statement
- repeating statement with high rise or (more sceptical) fall-rise
  You ˊsaw him?
- question tag with high rise or (more sceptical) fall-rise
  ˅Didn't you?
- **Are you quite sure (about that**/complement clause**)?**
  Are you quite sure you saw him?

1.4.6 asking for a piece of information
- *wh*-questions
- (event) **what happened?**
- (time) **when?**
  When will the guests arrive?
- (place) **where?**
  Where is my purse?
- (manner) **how?**
  How do you make an omelette?
- (degree) **how** + gradable adj/adv
  How far is it to York?
- (reason) **why?**
  Why are you here?
- *wh* **is it** + complement clause
  When is it your train leaves?
- **(Please) (can you) tell me** + NP/*wh*-clause
  Please can you tell me the way to the station?
  Tell me where you have been.

1.4.7 seeking identification
- **which?**
  Which one do you want?
- (of a person) **who?**
  Who is that lady?
- (of a person's occupation, nationality, etc.) **what?**
  What is her husband?
- (of possessor) **whose?**
  Whose gloves are these?

- **(of things, etc.) what?**
  What is this parcel?

1.4.8 asking for specification
- **what sort/kind of
  NP (+ VP + NP)?**
  What sort of animal was it?

1.4.9 expressing curiosity
- **I wonder**
  (+ *if*-clause/*wh*-clause)
  I wonder what he wants.
- **I'd like to know**
  (+ *if*-clause/*wh*-clause)
  I'd like to know if she was
  there.
- **question + I wonder
  (unstressed)?**
  Who is that, I wonder?

1.5 **answering questions**

1.5.1 confirming or disconfirming
- **Yes (+ positive tag)**
  Yes, I did.
- **No (+ negative tag)**
  No, I didn't.
- **I (don't) think so.**
- **I believe so/not.**
- **expressions of
  agreement/disagreement
  (2.1, 2.2)**
  Of course.
- **probability (2.3.1, 2.3.2)**
  Perhaps.
- **ignorance (2.2.3)**
  I don't know.
- **forgetting (2.2.4)**
  I don't remember.
- **certainty (2.2.7.1)**
  I'm not sure.

1.5.2. giving information
1.5.2.1 time
  (**e.g. in reply to** When will it
  happen?)
  - **temporal adverbs**
    Soon.

- **temporal phrases**
  Next Wednesday.
- **temporal clauses**
  When we're ready.

1.5.2.2 place
  (**e.g. in reply to** Where's my
  box?)
  - **locative adverbs**
    Here.
  - **locative phrases**
    On the table.
  - **locative clauses**
    Where you left it.

1.5.2.3 manner
  (**e.g. in reply to** How do you
  drive?)
  - **manner adverbs**
    Carefully.
  - **manner phrases**
    With care.

1.5.2.4 degree
  (**e.g. in reply to** How good is it?)
  - **adverb of degree + (adj/adv
    in question)**
    Very good.
  - **adj/adv expressing degree**
    Fair.

1.5.2.5 reason
  (**e.g. in reply to** Why are you
  here?)
  - **(because +) declarative
    sentence/of + NP**
    Because I'm a member and
    because of the meeting.

1.5.3 identifying
  (**e.g. in reply to** Which one do
  you want?)
  - **See 1.1.1 and 1.1.2.**
    That one. The large green one.

1.5.3.1 identifying a person
  (**e.g. in reply to** Who is that?)
  - **See 1.1.3.**
    It's me. John Smith.

1.5.3.2 identifying a person's
occupation, role, etc.
(e.g. in reply to What is she?)
- (personal pronoun + **be** +)
  NP denoting occupation
  role, etc.
  She's an actress.

1.5.3.3 identifying the possessor
(e.g. in reply to Whose are
these?)
- It's/they're + possessive
  pronouns (See Chapter 6,
  7.5.1.)
  They're mine.

1.5.3.4 identifying a thing
(e.g. in reply to What is this?)
- (It's/they're +) NP
  (non-human)
  It's my hat.

1.5.4 specifying
(e.g. in reply to What sort of
animal is this?)
- (It's/they're) + NP
  It's a grey squirrel.

1.5.5 questions asking for
confirmation, information,
identification or specification
can be answered by
expressions of ignorance (See
2.2.3.)
I haven't a clue.

2 Expressing and finding out attitudes

2.1 attitudes to matters of fact

2.1.1 expressing agreement with a
statement

2.1.1.1 expressing strong agreement
- **Exactly!**
- **Certainly!**
- **Absolutely!**
- **Definitely!**
- **Well said!**

- **Yes, indeed.**
- **I quite agree.**
- **You can say that again.**
- **Spot on!**
- **Just so.**
- (in public discussion) **Hear, hear!**

2.1.1.2 expressing agreement with a
positive statement
(e.g. with You work hard.)
- **Yes (+ positive tag)**
  Yes, we do.
- **(Certainly/Of course (+ tag)**
  Of course we do.
- **That's right.**
- **That's correct.**
- (more colloquial) **OK.**

2.1.1.3 expressing agreement with a
negative statement
(e.g. with You can't stop now.)
- **No (+ negative tag)**
  No, we can't.
- **Indeed not.**
- **Certainly not.**
- **Of course not.**

2.1.1.4 expressing reluctant
agreement
- **If you say so.**
- **I suppose so.**
- **No doubt.**

2.1.1.5 conceding a point
- **Good point.**
- **Fair enough.**

2.1.1.6 expressing agreement with
reservations
use of falling-rising
intonation
- **I a'gree with you ˇthere.**
- **I 'don't disa·gree with you
  ˇthere.**
- **'Up to a ˇpoint, ˎyes.**
- **That may 'well be ˇso, but ...**
- **Yes (+ tag with fall-rise)**
  ˇYes, it ˇis.

- I agree + complement clause (+ **but**)
  I a·gree that it's ˅difficult.
- **Perhaps so, but …**

2.1.1.7 demurring (See also 5.12.)
(e.g. in response to I think that's stupid.)
- **Well.**
- **Tag question**
  Is it?
- **I 'see what you ˅mean.** (fall-rise)

2.1.2 expressing disagreement with a statement
- **I don't agree.**
- **That's not right.**
- **You're wrong (there/about that).**

2.1.2.1 expressing strong disagreement
- **(Absolute) nonsense/rubbish.**
- **I couldn't agree less.**
- **No way!**
- **How can you (possibly) say that/such a thing?**

2.1.2.2 expressing disagreement with a positive statement
(e.g. Spinach is horrible.)
- **No (+ negative tag)**
  No. It isn't.
- **Not so.**
- **Certainly not.**
- **I don't think so.**

2.1.2.3 expressing disagreement with a negative statement
(e.g. Tomorrow isn't Wednesday.)
- **(Oh) Yes (+ positive tag)**
  Oh, yes it is.
- **I think + positive statement (with contrastive stress)**
  I think it's Wednesday tomorrow.

2.1.2.4 expressing weak disagreement
- **I can't/don't altogether agree.**
- **I'm not so sure.**
- **I wonder (if that is so).**

2.1.3 enquiring about agreement or disagreement
- **Do you agree?**
- **What do you think?**
- **statement + question tag (with rising intonation)**
  She is ˌFrench, | ˌisn't she?||

2.1.4 inviting agreement
- **(statement +) OK? (with high rise)**
  I ˌlike this ·music, O'K?
- **statement + question tag (with falling intonation)**
  She is ˌFrench, | ˌisn't she?||
- **Don't you agree (+ *that* clause)?**
  Don't you agree she's beautiful?
- **Don't you think (+ *that* clause)?**
  Don't you think it's nice?
- **Surely you agree (+ *that* clause)?**
  Surely you agree?
- **interrogative sentence with falling intonation**
  'Isn't she ˌlovely?

2.1.5 inviting disagreement with a statement
- **Surely you don't think + *that* clause**
  Surely you don't think it's cold?

2.1.6 denying statements (See also 2.1.2.1.)
(e.g. You were driving far too fast.)
- **That isn't true.**
- **That is (quite) untrue.**

- I deny it.
- That is a (downright) lie.
- Nonsense!
- Certainly/absolutely not.
- Not at all.
- (Most) certainly not.
- No (+ negative tag)
  No, I wasn't.
- negative sentences
  I didn't drive at all fast.

2.2 expressing knowledge, memory, belief

2.2.1 expressing knowledge (or not) of a person, thing or fact
- I (don't) know.
- I (don't) know + NP
  I know the way to your house.
- I (don't know) + wh-clause
  I don't know where he lives.
- I (don't) know + complement clause
  I know it's cold in winter.

2.2.2 asking about knowledge
- Do you know + NP?
  Do you know Mary Brown?
- Do you know + about NP?
  Do you know about his illness?
- Do you know + complement clause?
  Do you know that she's dead?
- Do you know + wh-clause?
  Do you know what he did?
- What do you know about + VPgerund?
  What do you know about mending furniture?
- Have you (ever) heard (+ of NP)?
  Have you ever heard of Livonia?
- Have you heard about NP?
  Have you heard about the bomb?
- Have you heard + complement clause?
  Have you heard that she's left him?
- Have you heard + wh-clause?
  Have you heard what happened today?
- You know (+ NP/complement clause/wh-clause) + tag question
  You know where he lives, don't you?

2.2.3 asserting ignorance
- I've no idea.
- I haven't a clue.
- negative expressions in 2.2.1
  I don't know.

2.2.4 expressing remembering or forgetting persons, things, facts and actions
- I (don't/can't) remember (+ NP)
  I remember our holiday in Spain.
- I (don't/can't) remember + VPgerund
  I don't remember saying that.
- I (don't/can't) remember + complement clause
  I remember that he gave it back.
- I (don't/can't) remember + wh-clause
  I can't remember where I left my handbag.
- I forget (+ wh-clause)
  I forget whether I've locked the door.
- I've/haven't forgotten (+ NP)
  I haven't forgotten my passport.

- **I've/haven't forgotten
+ VPgerund**
  I've never forgotten climbing
  Mont Blanc.
- **I've/haven't forgotten
+ to + VPinf**
  I've forgotten to lock the door.
- **I've/haven't forgotten
+ complement clause**
  I haven't forgotten that you're
  not well.
- **I've/haven't forgotten
+ *wh*-clause**
  I've forgotten where it is.

2.2.5 enquiring about
remembering and forgetting
- **Do(n't) you remember?**
- **Do(n't) you remember + NP?**
  Do you remember Capri?
- **Do(n't) you remember
+ VPgerund?**
  Don't you remember coming
  home last night?
- **Do(n't) you remember
+ complement clause?**
  Don't you remember that
  James was there too?
- **Do(n't) you remember
+ *wh*-clause?**
  Do you remember where you
  left it?
- **Have(n't) you remembered/
forgotten?**
- **Have(n't) you remembered/
forgotten + NP**
  Have you remembered her
  birthday?
- **Have(n't) you remembered/
forgotten + to + VPinf**
  Haven't you forgotten to feed
  the cat?
- **Have(n't) you remembered/
forgotten + complement
clause**
  Have you forgotten we're
  going out this evening?

- **Have(n't) you remembered
+ *wh*-clause**
  Haven't you remembered
  where we're going?

2.2.6 reminding someone
- **Don't forget**
- **(Please) remember/don't
forget + NP**
  Please remember the milk.
- **(Please) remember/don't
forget + to + VPinf**
  Don't forget to phone home.
- **(Please) remember/don't
forget + *wh*-clause**
  Please remember why we're
  here.
- **(Please) remember/don't
forget + complement clause**
  Please don't forget it's Sunday
  tomorrow.

2.2.7 expressing degrees of
certainty

2.2.7.1 confident assertion
- **in declarative sentences
certainly, definitely,
undoubtedly, beyond any
doubt**
  She is certainly over thirty.
- **I am (quite/absolutely)
certain/sure/convinced
(+ complement clause)**
  I am quite sure that Stalin died
  in 1952.
- **declarative sentences with
stressed *do, be* or auxiliary**
  I most certainly did post the
  letter.
- **declarative sentences
(+ tag) with low falling
intonation**
  'Ankara is in ˎTurkey.
- **I know (+ complement/*wh*-
clause)**
  I know Irún is in Spain, not
  France.

2.2.7.2 tentative assertion
- **NP + to seem/appear/look (+ to be) Adj/NP**
  The translation appears to be correct.
- **It seems/appears (to me) + complement clause**
  It seems to me that he was right.
- **It looks as if/as though + statement**
  It looks as if he's coming.
- **perhaps/maybe (also in declarative sentences)**
  Maybe you're right.
- **I (don't) think/ believe + so/complement clause**
  I don't think he's ever been here.
- **I'm not (quite/altogether) sure (+ but + tentative assertion)**
  I'm not quite sure, but I believe he's already gone.
- **declarative sentence + I think, with low rising intonation**
  He's ‚French, I ‚think.
- **I could be wrong, but + tentative statement**
  I could be wrong, but it looks as though they've won.

2.2.7.3 expressing uncertainty
- **I don't know (+ if-clause/wh-clause)**
  I don't know if he will come.
- **I'm not (at all) sure (+ if-clause/wh-clause/ complement clause)**
  I'm not at all sure what he wants.
- **I wonder (+ if-clause/wh-clause)**
  I wonder why they go into London by car.
- **I'm (very much) in two minds.**

2.2.7.4 expressing doubt, incredulity
- **I don't/can't believe + it/complement clause**
  I can't believe she's only thirty.
- **I (rather) doubt + it/if-clause**
  I rather doubt if he'll come.
- **Do you really think + so/complement clause?**
  Do you really think they'll agree?

2.2.7.5 expressing bewilderment
- **I'm puzzled.**
- **I'm (completely) baffled.**
- **This is beyond me.**
- **What does/can this mean?**
- **Don't ask me.**

2.2.7.6 enquiring about certainty
- **Are you sure (+ complement clause)**

2.3   expressing modality

2.3.1   expressing degrees of probability
Note Logically, probability (objective) is distinct from certainty (subjective). However, they correlate closely and some terms (e.g. *certain, perhaps*) may be used for both, since the confidence with which an assertion is made depends on the probability of it being true.

- **(absolutely) certain(ly)**
  He is certain to be there.
- **(most) probable/probably**
  That is the probable outcome.
- **NP + will/must (most) certainly/probably + VP**
  They will most probably lose.

- (quite) possible/possibly
  Defeat is certainly possible.
- NP + may/might/can/could+
  well/possibly/even/perhaps
  + VP
  Oxford may even win this year.
- (highly) improbable
  Rain in the Sahara is highly
  improbable,
- (totally) impossible
  but not totally impossible.
- NP + cannot possibly/
  conceivably + VP
  We cannot conceivably fail.
- (not) (very) likely/(very)
  unlikely
  That's not very likely.
- NP + be + certain/likely
  + to + VPinf
  The museum is likely to be
  closed.
- it is certain/probable/likely/
  possible/impossible
  + complement clause
  It is possible that he will resign.
- NP + will/must/may/might/
  can/cannot + VPinf
  That painting cannot be by
  Picasso.

2.3.2   enquiring about
        probability/possibility
- be + NP + certain/likely
  (+ to + VPinf)?
  Is Mary likely to come?
- Is it certain/probable/likely/
  possible/impossible
  + complement clause?
  Is it possible that you are
  mistaken?
- How certain/probable/
  likely/ possible is it
  + complement clause?
  How certain is it that it will
  rain?
- Will/must/may/might/can
  + NP + VPinf
  May Einstein be wrong?

- Sentences in 2.2.8 with high
  rising intonation on the
  word expressing
  probability.
  That ·painting 'cannot be by
  Pi·casso?

2.3.3   expressing necessity
        (including logical deduction)
- necessary/necessarily in
  declarative sentence
  Good shoes are necessarily
  expensive.
- NP + must/cannot + VPinf
  People must sleep sometimes.
- so/therefore + declarative
  sentence
  I think: therefore I exist.

2.3.4   denying necessity
- It isn't necessarily so.
- unnecessary/not necessary/
  not necessarily in
  declarative sentences
  A private car is not necessary in
  London.
- it is not necessary (+ for
  NP) + to + VPinf
  It is not necessary for guests to
  wear ties.
- NP + need not + VPinf
  Classical music need not be
  boring.

2.3.5   enquiring as to necessity
        (including logical deduction)
- Is that necessarily so?
- necessary/necessarily (in
  interrogative sentences)
  Are communists necessarily
  atheists?
- must/need + NP + VPinf?
  Must things be black or white?

2.3.6   expressing obligation
        (For moral obligation see
        2.6.1.)
- NP + have to/must + VPinf
  You must be home before
  midnight.

- **NP + must not + VPinf**
  You must not arrive late.

2.3.7   denying obligation
- **NP + do not have to/needn't
  + VPinf**
  You needn't say Sir to me off
  duty.

2.3.8   enquiring about obligation
- **(wh) do + NP + have
  to + VPinf**
  What do we have to say?
- **(wh) must + NP/VPinf**
  Must you go now?

**2.3.9   expressing ability to do
  something**
- **NP + can + VPinf**
  I can speak Spanish quite well.
- **NP + be + able to + VPinf**
  I am now able to tell you about
  it.

**2.3.10   denying ability to do
  something**
- **NP + cannot/can't + VPinf**
  You can't be in two places at
  the same time.
- **NP + be + not
  able/unable + to + VPinf**
  Sir Harold is unable to be
  present.

**2.3.11   enquiring about ability to do
  something**
- **interrogative sentences and
  wh-questions**
  Can you swim yet?
  corresponding to 2.3.9 and
  2.3.10
  Where can I find men's socks?

2.3.12   expressing permissibility
- **NP + be + allowed
  (+ adjunct)**
  Smoking is allowed in the bar.
- **NP + be + permitted
  (+ adjunct)**
  Parking is permitted after
  6 p.m.

- **NP + can/may + VPinf
  (+ adjunct)**
  Students may entertain guests
  until 11 p.m.

2.3.13   denying permissibility
- **NP + be + not allowed
  (+ adjunct)**
  Swimming is not allowed in
  this reservoir.
- **NP + be + not permitted
  (+ adjunct)**
  Photography is not permitted
  in the Cathedral.
- **NP + be (strictly) prohibited
  (+ adjunct)**
  Ball games are strictly
  prohibited.
- **NP + must not + VPinf**
  Children mustn't ever forget to
  say 'Please'.
- **NP + be + not
  supposed + VPinf**
  Visitors are not supposed to
  walk on the grass.

**2.3.14   enquiring about
  permissibility**
- **interrogative sentences and
  wh-questions
  corresponding to 2.3.12**
  Where may one park in the
  city?
  Can visitors enter the library?

**2.4   expressing and enquiring
  about volition**

**2.4.1   expressing wishes/wants/
  desires**
- **I'd like + NP**
  I'd like an income of £50,000 a
  year.
- **I'd like (NP) to + VPinf**
  I'd like to go and wash my
  hands.
- **I want + NP**
  I want a nice long holiday.
- **I want (NP) to + VPinf**
  I want you to give up smoking.

- I wish + complement clause
(note subjunctive were)
I wish I were twenty years
younger.

2.4.2 expressing negative wishes/
wants/desires
- **I'd like not to + VPinf**
I'd like not to have to work for
a living.
- **I don't want + NP**
I don't want any trouble.
- **I don't want to + VPinf**
I don't want to go to bed.
- **I wish + negative
complement clause**
I wish I weren't so fat.

2.4.3 enquiring about wishes/
wants/desires
- **What would you like
(+ adjunct)?**
What would you like for your
birthday?
- **What would you like to do?**
- **Would you like + NP**
Would you like a cake?
- **Would you like (+ NP) to
+ VPinf**
Would you like to come
fishing?
- **Do you want + NP**
Do you want anything?
- **Do you want (+ NP) to
+ VPinf**
Do you want me to try the suit
on?
- **What do you want?**
- **Is there anything you want?**

2.4.4 expressing intentions
- **NP + *be* + going to + VPinf**
I'm going to buy a new car.
- **NP + will + VPinf**
I will explain later.
- **NP + intend(s) to + VPinf**
Ann intends to go to America.

- **NP + *be* + thinking of
+ VPgerund**
We are thinking of driving to
Turkey.

2.4.5 expressing negative
intentions
- **I/we + *be* + not going
to + VPinf**
I'm not going to be beaten by
him.
- **I/we + won't + VPinf**
I won't stop trying.
- **I/we + *do* + not intend
to + VPinf**
I don't intend to resign.
- **I/we + *be* + not thinking
of + VPgerund**
We're not thinking of retiring
just yet.

2.4.6 enquiring about intentions
- **interrogative sentences and
wh-questions
corresponding to 2.4.4 and
2.4.5**
What are you going to do?
Will you fly to Geneva?
Aren't you thinking of coming
to bed?

2.5 **expressing and enquiring
about emotions**

2.5.1 expressing pleasure,
happiness
(with a smile, laughing, etc.)
- **This is/that's lovely/
wonderful/great/fine!**
- **How nice/delightful!**
- **I'm/I feel so happy!**
- **I'm really enjoying myself!**
- **Bliss!**
- **I'm delighted/(very) glad/
pleased
(+ to + VPinf/complement
clause)**
I'm very glad to see you here.

- It's a delight/(great) pleasure + to + VPinf
  It's a great pleasure to meet you.

2.5.2 expressing unhappiness, sadness
- Oh dear!
- I don't feel (at all) happy/ cheerful (today, etc.).
- I feel/am feeling (very) unhappy/miserable/ depressed/gloomy/upset/ sad.

2.5.3 enquiring about happiness/ unhappiness
- How are you (feeling) (today, etc.)?
- Are you happy/pleased?

2.5.4 enquiring about the cause of unhappiness/dissatisfaction/ disappointment
- What's the matter?

2.5.5 exhorting someone not to be dejected
- (Come on!) Cheer up!
- It's not the end of the world!
- Don't let it/them get you down!
- Never despair!
- Never mind!
- Better luck next time!

2.5.6 expressing regret/sympathy, condolence
- Oh dear!
- What a shame/pity (+ complement clause)
  What a pity Peter died so young.
- It's a great shame/pity (+ complement clause)
  It's a great shame you weren't there.
- I'm (so) (very) sorry (to hear + complement clause)
  I'm very sorry to hear you failed.

2.5.7 expressing fellow-feeling, empathy
- I know (just) how you feel.
- I (fully) sympathise.
- I feel (just) the same way.

2.5.8 expressing hope, expectation
- I (do) hope + complement clause
  I hope it stays fine.
- I hope/am hoping to + VPinf
  I hope to become a doctor.
- I (do) hope so.
- I (do) hope not.
- I am looking forward (greatly/very much) to + NP/VPgerund
  I'm looking forward very much to your visit.
- I am very excited about + NP/VPgerund
  I am very excited about your visit.

2.5.9 expressing disappointment
- I'm/I feel (very) disappointed.
- That's a (great) disappointment (to me).
- expressions and structures in 2.5.6

2.5.10 expressing fear/anxiety
- Help!
- I'm frightened/scared/ terrified/to death) (of NP)
  I'm scared to death of that man.
- I'm afraid (+ complement clause)
  I'm afraid he'll come back.
- I'm (too) afraid to + VPinf
  I'm afraid to complain about him.
- I'm (rather/very) worried/ anxious (+ about NP/ complement clause)
  I'm rather worried about Joan.

2.5.11 enquiring about fear/ anxiety/worry

- interrogative sentences and *wh*-questions corresponding to 2.5.10
  Are you afraid of the dark?
  Are you worried about your health?
- **Is something worrying you?**
- **Is there something on your mind?**
- **What's the matter?**
- **What are you afraid of?**
- **Why are you frightened/ worried?**

2.5.12 expressing pain, anguish, suffering

- **Oh!/Ow!/Ouch!**
- **That hurts!**
- **You're hurting me!**
- **I'm in (great) pain.**
- **My + NP body part hurts/is hurting/is (very) painful/is aching**
  My leg is hurting.
- **I've got a (bad) stomach-/headache**
- **I've got a (bad) pain in my NP body part**
  I've got a bad pain in my chest.

2.5.13 enquiring about pain, anguish, suffering

- **Have you got a pain/(stomach-/headache)?**
- **Does this/it hurt?**
- **Are you in (great) pain?**
- **When/where does it hurt?**
- **Where is the pain?**

2.5.14 reassuring a worried or frightened person, comforting a sufferer

- **There, there.**
- **'Don't ,worry. (with low rising intonation)**
- **'Don't be ,frightened. (with low rise)**

- **It's (·going to be) 'all ,right. (with low rise)**
- **Relax.**
- **Keep calm.**

2.5.15 expressing relief

- **Whew!**
- **Thank goodness (for that)!**
- **What a relief!**
- **That's a relief!**
- **Well, that's that!**

2.5.16 expressing liking, affection

- **NP + *be* + (very) good/nice/ pleasant**
  This coffee is very good.
- **I like/enjoy + NP/VPgerund (very much)**
  I like riding very much.
- **I have a great liking for NP/VPgerund**
  I have a great liking for Belgian chocolates.
- **I love/adore NP/VPgerund**
  I love cats.
- **I'm rather quite/very fond of NP/VPgerund**
  I'm very fond of my wife.
- **I feel great affection for NP**
  I feel great affection for Florence.

2.5.17 expressing dislike

- **Ugh!**
- **NP/VPgerund + *be* + not (very/at all) good/nice/ pleasant**
  These cakes are not very nice.
- **NP + *be* + (rather/very) nasty/horrible/awful/ unpleasant bad**
  His views are rather nasty.
- **I don't like/enjoy NP/VPgerund (very much/at all)**
  I don't like sweet tea at all.
- **I hate/detest/dislike + NP/VPgerund**
  I hate saying no to people.

- **I (simply) can't stand NP/VPgerund**
  I can't stand hypocrisy.

2.5.18 enquiring about like and dislike
- **What do you think of NP/VPgerund?**
  What do you think of this wine?
- **Do you like/enjoy NP/VPgerund?**
  Do you enjoy ballet?
- **How do you like NP/VPgerund?**
  How do you like playing pop music?
- **What do you (dis)like (doing)?**
- **Who/what is your favourite NP?**
  Who is your favourite film star?
- **What is your pet aversion?**

2.5.19 expressing preference
- **I prefer + NP/VPgerund (+ to NP/VPgerund)**
  I prefer hockey to football.
- **I'd rather + VPinf (than + contrastive element)**
  I'd rather travel by train than by car.
- **I like NP/VPgerund better than NP/VPgerund**
  I like brandy better than sherry.
- **I think NP/VPgerund is better than/preferable to + NP/VPgerund**
  I think winning is better than losing.

2.5.20 enquiring about preference
- **interrogative sentences and wh-questions corresponding to 2.5.19**
  Do you prefer coffee to tea?
  Which brand do you prefer?
  Do you like cats better than dogs?

- **Which do you prefer: NP/VPgerund or NP/VPgerund?**
  Which do you prefer: Scotch or Irish?
- **NP or NP?**
  Coffee or tea?
- **Adj or Adj?**
  Black or white?
- **Prep or Prep?**
  With or without?
- **Adv or Adv?**
  Now or later?

2.5.21 expressing satisfaction
- **Good!/Fine!/Excellent!**
- **Just right!**
- **demonstrative (+ NP) + *be* + (very) good/nice**
  That pudding was very nice.
- **(demonstrative (+ NP) + *be*) + just what I want(ed)/need(ed)/meant/had in mind**
  This is just what I had in mind.
- **(following dissatisfaction)**
- **That's much better.**
- **That's OK (now).**
- **It's (quite) all right (now).**
- **Right-ho.**
- **That'll do.**
- **That's (good) enough.**

2.5.22 expressing dissatisfaction
- **declarative sentences (reporting cause of dissatisfaction)**
  This soup is cold.
  The TV doesn't work.
- **I'm not satisfied/happy (with + NP)**
  I'm not happy with this fridge.
- **I don't like/want + NP**
  I don't want this soap.
- **I don't like/want + NP like this**
  I don't like cabbage like this.

- NP + **be** + (still)
  not + right/good (yet)
  The sound is still not right.
- This/these + **be** + not what I
  want(ed)/need(ed)/meant/
  had in mind/asked for
  This is not what I meant.
- This/that will not do.
- This/that is not good
  enough.

2.5.23 enquiring about
satisfaction/dissatisfaction
- Is everything all right/OK/in
  order?
- Are you (quite) satisfied/
  happy (with + NP)
  Are you quite satisfied with
  your meal?
- Do you like NP like this?
  Do you like coffee like this?
- Is it all right/OK (now)?
- Will this do?
- Is this what you want(ed)/
  need(ed)/meant/had in
  mind/asked for?
- Is everything to your
  satisfaction?
- How do you like/find NP?
  How do you find our beer?
- Is anything the matter?
- Is anything wrong?
- What's the matter/problem?
- What's wrong?

2.5.24 complaining
- I have a complaint (to make).
- I'm sorry, but . . .
- I don't want to complain,
  but . . .
  Then expressions and
  structures as per 2.5.22

2.5.25 expressing bad temper
- I'm in a bad mood/temper
  (just now/today).

- I'm/I feel (rather/quite/very)
  cross/angry/livid/annoyed/
  irritated (with + NP/about
  + NP)
  I feel very angry about the new
  road.
- NP + **be** (very) annoying/
  irritating/infuriating
  John is being very annoying.
- It's enough to drive you
  mad/try the patience of a
  saint.

2.5.26 reacting to bad temper
- Calm down!
- Don't get so angry/worked
  up!
- There's nothing to get angry
  about.
- There's no need to be so
  impatient/take offence.
- Don't take it to heart/the
  wrong way.
- It's a storm in a teacup.
- Don't make a mountain out
  of a molehill.

2.5.27 apologising for bad temper
- I'm sorry I lost control/
  patience/my temper.
- No hard feelings (I hope/
  trust).

2.5.28 expressing interest
- Really!
- Fascinating!
- Is that so!
- Well, well.
- (How) (very) interesting!
- I am (very) interested in
  NP/VPgerund
  I am interested in old stamps.
- NP interest(s) me (greatly)
  Greek men interest me greatly.

2.5.29 expressing lack of interest
- (How) boring!
- I am (utterly) bored (by NP/VPgerund)
  I am utterly bored by politics on TV.
- I am not (very/at all) interested in NP/VPgerund
  I am not at all interested in going abroad.
- NP/VPgerund does not interest me (very much/at all)
  Sport does not interest me at all.

2.5.30 expressing surprise
- Good Lord/Heavens!
- What a ('nice) sur`prise! (with high fall)
- How sur`prising! (with high fall)
- (Just) Fancy `that/VPgerund! (with high fall)
  Just 'fancy ·swimming at `Christmas!
- Well, this is a surprise.
- (That is/I find that) very surprising.
- I'm surprised (to hear) (+ complement clause) (unpleasant)
  It surprises me that the dollar is so weak.
- What a shock!
- Oh, no!
- How awful/dreadful
- That comes as a (complete) shock (to me)

2.5.31 enquiring about surprise
- Does(n't) that surprise you?
- Is(n't) this/that what you expected/were expecting?
- Are(n't) you surprised (+ complement clause)
  Aren't you surprised that I came to see you?
- Do(n't) you find it surprising (+ complement clause)
  Don't you find it surprising that he hasn't said anything yet?

2.5.32 expressing lack of surprise
- 'Well? (with high rise)
- Sur'prise, sur`prise! (ironic)
- Just what you might expect.

2.5.33 expressing indifference
- So what!
- I don't mind care (+ if clause)
  I don't care if it is foggy or fine.
  It is all the same to me.
- I couldn't care less.
- It is nothing to me.
- It leaves me cold.
- What is that to me?

2.3.34 enquiring about indifference
- Don't you care?
- Is it nothing to you (+ complement clause)?
  Is it nothing to you that people are starving?

2.5.35 expressing fatigue, resignation
- I'm (rather/very) tired.
- I've had enough.
- I'm worn out.
- There's nothing (more) to be done.
- There's nothing (more) I can do.
- Leave it.

2.5.36 expressing gratitude
- Thank you (so much/very much (indeed))
- (Many) thanks
- It/That was (so/very/most) kind/nice/good of you (to + VPinf)
  It was most kind of you to call.
- I'm (very) grateful to you (for NP/VPgerund)
  I'm very grateful to you for telling me about it.

2.5.37 reacting to an expression of gratitude
- **Thank you (with stress on *you*)**
- **Not at all.**
- **It is/was/has been a pleasure.**

2.6   expressing moral attitudes

2.6.1 expressing moral obligation
- **NP + *be* (not) supposed to + VPinf**
  You are not supposed to do that.
- **NP + should(n't)/ought (not) to + VPinf**
  Motorists ought to drive more slowly.
- **It is (not) right wrong to + VPinf**
  It is not right to cheat.
- **NP/VPgerund is (not) right/wrong**
  Eating people is wrong.

2.6.2 expressing approval
- **(very) good**
- **(That's) fine excellent!**
- **Well done!**
- **Good show!**
- **I (strongly) approve (of + NP/noun clause)**
  I strongly approve of what you have done.
- **NP + *be* (quite) right (to + VPinf)**
  You were quite right to object.

2.6.3 expressing disapproval, protest
- **Tut-tut. (clicks)**
- **Bad show.**
- **That's/It's not (very) good/ nice.**
- **You ought not to have done it/that.**
- **You shouldn't have done it/that.**
- **You ought to be ashamed of yourself.**

- **I (strongly) disapprove (of + NP/VPgerund)**
  I strongly disapprove of gambling.
- **I don't/can't approve of NP/noun clause**
  I can't approve of adultery.
- **I'm against/not in favour of NP/VPgerund**
  I'm not in favour of legalising drugs.
- **(in public meetings) Shame!**
- **I (must) protest (against NP/VPgerund)**
  I must protest against this decision.

2.6.4 enquiring about approval/disapproval
- **(Is this) OK/all right?**
- **How's this?**
- **Do you approve (of + NP/VPgerund)?**
  Do you approve of smoking?
- **What do you think of NP/VPgerund?**
  What do you think of the Lottery?
- **How do you find NP/VPgerund?**
  How do you find living in England?

2.6.5 attaching/accepting blame
- **It's (all) NP's fault.**
  It's all my fault.
- **NP + *be* + to blame (for NP/VPgerund)**
  You are to blame for the accident.

2.6.6 denying blame
- **It isn't/wasn't my fault.**
- **I + *be* + not to blame (for NP/VPgerund)**
  I am not to blame for losing the match.
- **I + *be* (entirely) innocent**
  I am innocent.

2.6.7 apologising, asking
forgiveness
- **(I'm) (so/very) sorry (for
NP/VPgerund)**
Sorry for the chaos.
- **Please forgive me (for
NP/VPgerund)**
Please forgive me for shouting
at you.
- **I (do) apologise (for
NP/VPgerund)**
I do apologise for arriving so
late.

2.6.8 apologising for disturbing
somebody
- **I beg your pardon.**
- **Excuse me, please.**

2.6.9 accepting an apology,
granting forgiveness
- **Not at all.**
- **That's (quite) all right.**
- **It doesn't matter (at all/one
bit).**
- **Forget it.**
- **No problem.**
- **I forgive you.**
- **Let bygones be bygones.**

3   Deciding on and
managing courses of
action: Suasion

3.1   **suggesting a joint course of
action (involving both
speaker and addressee)**
- **Let's + VPinf!**
Let's go!
- **Shall we + VPinf?**
Shall we dance?
- **We could/might (perhaps)**
We might perhaps go by train.
- **What/How about
+ NP/VPgerund**
How about walking home?
- **Why not + VPinf?**
Why not fly there?

- **Why don't we + VPinf?**
Why don't we ask them to
dinner?

3.2   **agreeing to a suggestion**
- **Yes, let's.**
- **Why not, (indeed)?**
- **(That's a) (very) good idea.**
- **Certainly.**

3.3   **requesting someone to do
something**

3.3.1 urgent requests
- **VP imperative**
Stop! Don't move! Stand
back!
- **You must + VPinf (stress on
must)**
You *must* stop now.

3.3.2 giving instructions and orders
- **VP imperative**
Add flour and milk and stir
continuously.
- **You + VP simple present**
You turn right at the
crossroads and carry straight
on.
- **We shall/you will + VPinf**
We shall meet here at the same
time tomorrow.
- **Will you + VPinf (please)
(falling intonation)**
'Will you ·stop ˌtalking now,
·please.
(more insistent)
- **Will you please + VPinf
(falling)**
·Will you 'please ·stop ˌtalking.
- **VP imperative (please)**
Stop talking, please.
- **Do (please) VPinf (will you
unstressed)**
'Do ·stop ˌtalking, ·will you?

3.3.3 ordering goods/a meal/a drink/etc.
- **I'd like/give me/I'll have + NP (please after last item only)**
  A large brown loaf. And I'll have six rolls, please.

3.3.4 asking someone for something
- **I'd (very much) like + NP (please)**
  I'd like a gin and tonic, please.
- **Please may I have + NP**
  Please may I have a piece of cake?
- **Can/could I have + NP (please)**
  Could I have a smaller piece, please?
- **Do you think I could have + NP please**
  Do you think I could have my tea without sugar, please?

3.3.5 making polite requests
- **Please + VP imperative**
  Please sit down.
- **VP imperative, please**
  Come in, please.
- **Would/can/could you (be so kind as to) VPinf, please**
  Could you close the door, please?
- **Do/would you mind + VPgerund, please**
  Would you mind waiting, please?
- **I wonder if/do you think you could (be so kind as to VPinf), please**
  I wonder if you could be so kind as to open the window, please.

3.3.6 dropping hints for someone to act on
- declarative sentences + tag (falling)
  It's ˋcold in here. ǀ ˋisn't it?ǁ

- **It would be nice + *if*-clause**
  It would be nice if someone could shut the window.
- **I don't suppose + complement clause (falling-rising)**
  I 'don't suppose ·someone could ·light the ˇfire? ˙

3.3.7 pleading
- **Please (high fall) + VP imperative (rising)**
  ˋPlease don't ˌhurt me.

3.3.8 asking for assistance
- **Help!**
- **Can/could you help me, please?**
- **Do you think you could give/lend me a hand?**

3.4 **responding to a request**

3.4.1 agreeing to a request willingly
- **Certainly.**
- **Willingly.**
- **With pleasure.**
- **It's a pleasure.**
- **Yes (of course) I will.**

3.4.2 agreeing with reservations
- **ˇYes. with falling-rising intonation**
- **Yes + *if*-clause**
  Yes, if I can.
- **Only + *if*-clause**
  Only if it's not raining.
- **Not + *unless*-clause**
  Not unless you pay me.

3.4.3 agreeing with reluctance
- **Well, all right.**
- **If you like.**
- **If I must.**
- **If you insist.**
- **I suppose I'd better.**
- **I don't mind.**

3.4.4 demurring
- ˅Well (with falling-rising intonation)
- I don't (really) know (if I can).
- I'd ˅like to (with fall-rise), but (+ declarative sentence)
  I'd like to, but I don't know if I could spare the time.
- I'll see (what I can do).
- I can't promise.

3.4.5 refusing
- No way!
- Sorry.
- No. (I'm sorry but) I can't.
- (I'm afraid) it's impossible/out of the question.
- Not a hope.
- I'm sorry, but I'm afraid I don't see how I can.

3.4.6 expressing defiance

3.4.6.1 defiance of an order
- (Oh) no I won't.
- Never!

3.4.6.2 defiance of a prohibition
- (Oh) yes I will.
- Just you try to stop me.

3.4.6.3 defiance of a stated intention
- Don't you dare!
- Just you try!
- Over my dead body!
- No way!

3.5 offering assistance
- Let me help you.
- Can I help you?
- Can/shall I give/lend you a hand?
- Can I do anything to help?
- Can I be of assistance?
- What can I do for you?
- Can you manage?

3.6 giving advice
- You should + VPinf
  You should go to the police.
- You (really) ought to + VPinf
  You really ought to be more careful.
- Why don't you + VPinf
  Why don't you stop working so hard?
- If I were you I'd + VPinf
  If I were you I'd phone him now.
- You could (always) try + VPgerund
  You could always try sending a fax.

3.7 giving warnings
- VP imperative with falling-rising intonation
  Be ˅careful! 'Look ˅out!
- Watch out (for NP)
  Watch out for that hole!
- Don't + VPinf (with fall-rise)
  'Don't ˅cut your·self!
- Mind + NP
  Mind your head!
- declarative sentences with fall-rise
  That ·knife is ˅sharp!

3.8 giving encouragement
- Come on (+ VP imperative)
  Come on.
- Now then (+ VP imperative)
  Now then, don't stop.
- Keep it up!
- Keep (on) + VPgerund
  Keep on trying.
  (See also 2.5.5.)

3.9 asking permission
- Can/could/may/might I (+ VPinf) (please)
  Can I come in? May I?
- Do you mind (+ *if*-clause) (please)
  Do you mind if I sit down?

- **Is it all right** (+ *if*-clause)
  Is it all right if I smoke?
- **Do you think I could/ might + VPinf (please)**
  Do you think I could go now, please?

3.10 granting permission

3.10.1 granting permission willingly
- **Yes.**
- **Certainly.**
- **Please do.**
- **By all means.**
- **Of course.**
- **That's (quite) all right (by me).**

3.10.2 granting permission with reservations
- **ᵛYes (with falling-rising intonation)**
- **(Yes +)** *if*-clause
  Yes. If you're quick about it.
- **(Yes +) provided + complement clause**
  Provided you don't stay out too late.
- **Not +** *unless*-clause
  Not unless you promise to help me clear up afterwards.

3.10.3 granting permission with reluctance
- **If you must.**
- **I suppose so.**
- **I 'can't ˏstop you (ˏcan I?) (with falling intonation)**
- **'If you ˏlike (with low rise)**
- **(advising not to do it) You 'can if you ᵛlike (with fall-rise on like)**
- **expressions in 3.4.3**

3.10.4 demurring
- **expressions as in 3.4.4**

3.11 refusing or withholding permission
e.g. in reply to Can I park here?
- **No** (+ negative tag)
  No, you can't.
- **ᵛSorry (with fall-rise)**
- **I'm afraid not.**
- **I'm ᵛsorry (with fall-rise) +** *but*-clause
  I'm ᵛsorry, but it's 'not alˏlowed.
- **Not + adverbial(s)**
  Not here until 6.30 p.m.

3.12 prohibiting someone from doing something
- **Don't** (+ VPinf)
  Don't walk on the ice.
- **You mustn't can't** (+ VPinf)
  You can't smoke in here.
- **(strongly expressed) Don't you dare** (+ VPinf)
  Don't you dare come in here with dirty boots on.
- **(more formal) I forbid you to** + VPinf
  I forbid you to see any more of him.
- **I cannot allow you to** + VPinf
  I cannot allow you to waste your time like this.
- **(at a meeting) I (must) veto this proposal.**

3.13 offering to do something for someone
- **Can I do anything for you?**
- **Can/Shall I** + VPinf (for you)?
  Shall I wash up for you?
- **Would you like me to** + VPinf (for you)?
  Would you like me to tell you a story?
  (pressing offers)
- **Do let me** + VPinf (for you)
  Do let me carry that case.
- **You must let me** + VPinf (for you)
  You must let me babysit for you.

3.14 offering somebody something
- **Would you like + NP?**
  Would you like a biscuit?
- **Can I/Let me offer you + NP**
  Let me offer you a lift.
- **(Do) have + NP**
  Do have another.
- **How about + NP**
  How about a gin and tonic?

3.15 inviting someone to do something
- **(How) would you like to + VPinf**
  How would you like to come sailing?
- **What/How about + VPgerund**
  What about having lunch together?

3.15.1 (pressing invitations)
- **(Do +) VP imperative**
  Do spend a weekend at our place.
- **You (simply) must + VPinf**
  You must come to dinner with us.

3.15.2 (tentative invitations)
- **You wouldn't like to VPinf, would you?**
  You wouldn't like to stay with us, would you?
- **I don't suppose you'd like to VPinf, would you?**
  I don't suppose you'd like to come to the opera, would you?

3.16 declining an offer or invitation

3.16.1 firm refusal
- **No, thank you.**
- **(I'm sorry but) I can't (+ VPinf)**
  I'm sorry but I can't come that day.

- **It's very good/kind of you (to offer/invite us) + *but*-clause**
  It's very good of you, but my wife is ill.
- **Unfortunately I can't (+ VPinf)**
  Unfortunately, I can't eat cheese.
- **I'm afraid I can't (+ VPinf)**
  I'm afraid I can't leave the dog.

3.16.2 demurring or weak refusal (inviting renewal of offer/invitation)
- **I don't think I really ought to.**
- **I don't want to put you to any trouble.**
- **Are you sure (+ complement clause)?**
  Are you sure it's convenient?
- **I don't really know (whether I can)**
- **I'd ˅like to, but … (with fall-rise)**

3.17 enquiring whether an offer or invitation is accepted
- **ˊCan/ˊwill you + VPinf (after all)? (with high rise)**
  ˊWill you be ·coming to ·dinner after ·all?
- **Do you know (yet) whether you can/will + VP (after all)**
  Do you know yet whether you can come?

4 Socialising

4.1 attracting attention
- **Excuse me.**
- **Hallo.**
- **I say …**

4.2 greeting people

4.2.1 greeting strangers and acquaintances
- **Good morning/ afternoon/evening (+ address form)**
- **(less formal) Hallo**

4.2.2 greeting friends and close acquaintances
- **Hallo + address form**
- **How *are* you (stress on *are*)?**
- **(informal) How are you doing/keeping/getting on?**

4.3 replying to a greeting

4.3.1 (if in normal health)
- **(I'm) fine/very well (thank you). How are *you* (stress on *you*)?**

4.3.2 (if in poor health)
- **Well, so-so (thank you). How are *you*?**

4.3.3 (if recovering from an illness, etc.)
- **(Much) better, thank you. How are *you*?**

4.4 address forms

4.4.1 addressing a friend or relative
- **first name**
  Hallo John. How are you keeping?

4.4.2 addressing an acquaintance
- **formal title (+ family name)**
  Yes, Dr Robinson.
- **honorific (Mr, Mrs, Miss) + family name**
  Good morning. Mrs Jones, how are you today?
- **Sir + first name**
  Yes, Sir John.

4.4.3 addressing a stranger (official, customer, member of public, etc.)

4.4.3.1 formal address
- **formal title (Professor/Doctor/Officer/ Captain, etc.)**
  I was driving at 30 m.p.h., Officer.
- **Sir/madam**
  That will be £35, Sir.

4.4.3.2 informal address
- **no address form**
  Hallo, can I help you?

4.4.4 terms of endearment
- **(My) dear/darling/love**

4.5 making introductions

4.5.1 formal introductions
- **address form + may I introduce + honorific**
  Professor Smith, may I introduce Dr Anthony Brown?
- **address form + I'd like you to meet + first name + family name**
  Mrs Alexander, I'd like you to meet Jonathan Prior.

4.5.2 informal introductions
- **address form + this is + first name + family name**
  Jane, this is John Hargreaves. **(especially among young people on social occasions)**
- **first name + meet + first name (and reverse)**
  Jenny, meet Bill: Bill, meet Jenny.

4.5.3 introducing oneself

4.5.3.1 (more formal)
- **(Good morning/afternoon/ evening) How do you do?**
  How do you do? My name is James Scott.
  I'm/My name is + first name + family name

4.5.3.2 (informal)
- Hallo. I'm + first name
  (+ family name)
  Hallo, I'm Ted.

4.5.4 when being introduced or
when someone is introduced
to you

4.5.4.1 formal
- How do you do.

4.5.4.2 informal
- Hallo.
- (It's) good/(I'm) (very)
  pleased to meet you.

4.5.5 enquiring whether an
introduction is needed
- Do you know each other?
- Address form, do you
  know + honorific/first
  name + family name
  Miss Jones, do you know
  Captain Clark?
- I think you (two) know each
  other (don't you).
- Have you already met?

4.6 making someone welcome
e.g. on entry into someone's
home
- Welcome!
- Do come in.
- Make yourself at home.

4.7 at a meal

4.7.1 before eating
- no special greeting

4.7.2 inviting guests to serve
themselves
- Please help yourself.

4.8 proposing a toast
- Cheers!
- Your (very) good health.
- Here's to + NP
  Here's to the bride and groom!

4.9 congratulating someone
- (Many) congratulations!
- Well done!
- Brilliant!
- (in sports) Well + past
  participle
  Well run! Well played!

4.10 good wishes

4.10.1 on someone's birthday
- Many happy returns (of the
  day)!
- Happy birthday!

4.10.2 at festival times
- Merry Christmas!
- Happy New Year!

4.10.3 wishing someone success
- Good/the best of luck!
- (I) hope it/all goes well!
- Cross fingers!

4.10.4 when someone is going out,
or on holiday
- Enjoy yourself/yourselves!
- Have a good time!

4.10.5 when parting from someone
- All the best!
- Keep well.
- Look after yourself.
- Take care.
- (Do) keep in touch.
- Let's be hearing from you.
- Have a good journey/
  trip/holiday.

4.11 taking leave

4.11.1 formal leave taking
- 'Good + ˌmorning/
  afterˌnoon/ˌevening/ˌnight
  (+ address form)
  (with low rising intonation)

4.11.2 informal
- It's been nice meeting you.
- See you again soon.

- See you/be seeing you
  (+ temporal adverbial)
  See you next week.
- Goodbye for now.

4.11.3 colloquial
- So long.
- Bye-bye!
- Cheerio!

4.11.4 if you are not expecting to meet again
- Goodbye.

5 Structuring discourse

5.1 opening
(See also 4.1, 4.2, 4.4.)

5.1.1 on formal occasions
- Ladies and gentlemen!

5.1.2 as participant in a meeting
- Mr/Madam Chairman
- Chair(person)

5.1.3 informally
- Right (now)!
- Well (now)
- Ahem (sound of clearing one's throat)

5.2 introducing a theme

5.2.1 at the start of a discourse
- To begin/start with, I'd like to + VPinf
  To begin with, I'd like to tell you why I'm here.

5.2.2 introducing a topic
- Now, I'd like to say something about + NP
  Now, I'd like to say something about the problem of pollution.

5.2.3 introducing a report/narrative or description
- I'd like to tell you about NP
  I'd like to tell you about a friend of mine.

- I'd like to tell you
  + wh-clause
  I'd like to tell you what happened to me the other day.

5.2.4 introducing an anecdote
- There was this NP
  There was this Englishman who had never been abroad before.

5.3 expressing an opinion
- As I see it + declarative sentence
  As I see it, terrorists are murderers.
- In my opinion + declarative sentence
  In my opinion, most TV programmes are boring.
- (Personally) I think
  + complementary clause
  I think we should go now.
- If you ask me, + declarative sentence
  If you ask me, they are all alike.

5.4 enumerating
- In the first place ..., in the second place ... (etc.)
  In the first place, smoking is bad for you: in the second place, it smells unpleasant.
- First ... second(ly) + third(ly) ..., (etc.)
  First, it's a good idea; secondly, it works.
- First ... then ... then ...,
  (etc.)
  First order, then eat, then pay, then leave.
- ... and ... and ...
  Mix together flour, and eggs, and milk.
- For one thing ...: for another ...
  For one thing, he's too fat; for another, he's too old.

5.5 exemplifying

- **for example**
  Many men – John for example – are rather shy.
- **(in written texts) e.g.**
  Visas are required for many countries, e.g. Russia and Turkey.
- **for instance**
  I can't eat fish. Prawns, for instance, make me sick.
- **…etcetera (in writing) etc.**
  Avoid shellfish; mussels, oysters, etc.
- **…and so on**
  She likes old cities: Florence, Segovia, and so on.

5.6 emphasising

- **word order**
  Now this picture I like very much.
- **use of adverbs of degree: especially/extremely/ particularly/very (very), etc.**
  These cakes are especially nice.
- **(please) note + NP/noun clause**
  Please note that we are closed on Mondays.
- **It is important to + VPinf**
  It is important to keep the door closed.
- **I must emphasise/stress (the fact) + *that*-clause**
  I must stress the fact that fire is dangerous.

5.6.1 in speech

- **use of strong stress**
  This man is *dangerous*.
- **use of high falling nucleus**
  It's ʹ*really* ʹgreat.
- **use of fall-rise in subordinate groups**
  In ˅summer, it's O˅K. In ˅winter, it's ʹhell.

5.6.2 in writing

- **NB**
  NB No collection is made on bank holidays.

5.6.2.1 emphasis in hand- or type-written texts

- use of underlining
  He is very unreliable.
- devices as in 5.6.1 as appropriate

5.6.2.2 emphasis in printed or word-processed texts

- use of italics
  Items are priced
  before tax.
- use of bolding
  This document is **highly confidential.**
- use of capitals
  Do NOT park here.

5.7 defining

- **that is/means (to say)**
  He is very discreet. That is to say, he will not talk unless told to.
- **(in writing) i.e.**
  They say he is given to paronomasia (i.e. punning).

5.8 summarising

- **to sum up**
- **in brief…**
- **to cut a long story short…**
- **all in all…**

5.9 changing the theme

- **(Now) to change the subject,**
- **Now for something different.**
- **To pass on to something else,**
- **I have another point (to make).**

5.10   **asking someone to pass to a new theme**
- I'd like to ask you something else.

5.11   **asking someone's opinion**
- What do you think (about/of NP)?
  What do you think of pop music?
- What is your opinion/view?
- Where do you stand (on NP/this matter)?
  Where do you stand on abortion?
- How do you see it?
- How does it look/seem from your point of view?

5.12   **showing that one is following a person's discourse**
- I see.
- ,Yes/,No (with low rise)
- ,Uh-huh (with low rise)
- Really?
- Oh!
- Indeed.
- Tag questions
  Is she?
- Is that so?
- How interesting.

5.13   **interrupting, asking for the floor**
- Excuse me.
- May I come in here?
- May I say something?
- One moment, please.
- Can/may I put my side of the case?
- May I speak (now)?

5.14   **objecting/protesting**
- No, I'm sorry but …
  No, I'm sorry but that isn't true.
- I (must strongly) object!
- I must protest (in the strongest possible terms).
- That is (quite) unacceptable.

- I can't accept that.
- I can't let you get away with that.

5.15   **asking someone to be silent**
- Sh!
- Quiet, please.
- (strongly expressed) Shut up!
- (colloquial) Pipe down!

5.16   **indicating a wish to continue**
- Just one moment/a minute, please.
- Please let me finish.
- As I was saying …
- (Please) don't/do not interrupt.
- I have just one thing left to say.

5.17   **encouraging someone to continue**
- (Do) go on (please).

5.18   **indicating that one is coming to an end**
- Finally …
- To finish/in conclusion, I should like to say …

5.19   **closing**

5.19.1   at the end of a speech
- Thank you for your attention.

5.19.2   at the end of a conversation
- Well, it's been nice talking (to/with you).
- See also 4.11.

5.20   **using the telephone (in addition to 5.1–19)**

5.20.1   opening the conversation by answering the call
- giving the telephone number
  (Oxford) five oh two double one.

- **Hallo?**
- **Hallo. (this is) + personal name (speaking/here)**
  Hallo, this is Mary Smith speaking.
  Hallo, Henry Bloggs here.

5.20.2 response by initiator of call
- **personal name + here**
  Marcel Leblanc here.
- **Hallo + address form (+ this is) + own name (+ speaking)**
  Hallo Mary, this is Günther Schmidt speaking.
- **(if number unidentified) Hallo, is that + personal name/company, etc. name**
  Hallo, is that Berkshire Motors?

5.20.3 asking for

5.20.3.1 a person
- **(Can I speak to +) personal name + please?**
  Can I speak to George, please?
- **(more formal) Could you put me through to + personal name, please?**
  Could you put me through to Mr Oakham, please?

5.20.3.2 an extension
- **(Can I have) extension + number + please**
  Can I have extension one oh six, please?

5.20.4 verifying caller
- **Who is that calling, please?**

5.20.5 asking someone to wait
- **Hold the line, please.**
- **Just a moment, please.**
- **The line/extension is engaged. Will you wait?**

5.20.6 asking whether one is heard and understood
- **Hallo?**

- **Are you (still) there?**
- **Can you (still) hear me?**

5.20.7 announcing new call
- **I'll call back (again) (+ temporal adverbial)**
  I'll call back later, when it's more convenient.

5.20.8 signing off signals
- **I must go now.**
- **Thank you for calling.**
- **expressions as in 4.10 and 4.11**

5.21 letters (in addition to 5.1–19)

5.21.1 opening formulae

5.21.1.1 to strangers whose name is not known, companies, etc.
- **Dear Sir/Madam,**

5.21.1.2 to acquaintances and named strangers
- **Dear + honorific + family name**
  Dear Professor Jones

5.21.1.3 to family friends and closer acquaintances
- **Dear + first name (or nickname if appropriate)**
  Dear Dick
- **My dear + first name**
  My dear Harry

5.21.1.4 on terms of endearment only
- **(My) Dearest + first name**
  My dearest Helen
- **Darling (+ first name)**
  Darling George

5.21.2 closing formulae

5.21.2.1 following 5.21.1.1
- **Yours faithfully**
  Yours faithfully
  normal signature
  printed form of signature
  J.L.M. Trim

5.21.2.2 following 5.21.1.2
- **Yours sincerely**
  Yours sincerely
  normal signature
  (if normal signature
  unrecognisable to
  recipient)
  printed form of signature
  J.L.M. Trim
- **Yours sincerely**
  Yours sincerely
  first name + family name
  John Trim

5.21.2.3 following 5.21.1.3
- **(friends) (With) all best wishes**
  first name only
- **close friends Yours ever**
- **family and close friends (With) love**

5.21.2.4 following 5.21.1.4
- **With (all my/very best) love**
- **personalised endings**

6 Assuring and repairing communication

6.1 signalling non-understanding
- ʹSorry? (with high rise)
- (Sorry (with fall-rise)) I don't (quite) understand
- (+ that word)
- (+ that expression)
- (+ what you said)
- (+ repetition of item not understood)
  ʵSorry, || ʹdon't underʹstand ,brill. ||

6.2 asking for repetition

6.2.1 of the whole utterance
- I ʹbeg your pardon (with high rise)?

- ʹWhat did you ·say, ·please (with high rise on *what*)?
- (Sorry), could you say that again, please?
- (Sorry), could you repeat that (for me), (please)?

6.2.2 of a particular word or phrase
- (Sorry +) *wh*-question with high rise on *wh* word
  ʵSorry, ʹwhere does he ·live?
- (Sorry +) indirect *wh*-question, including **did you say** with high rise on *wh* word
  ʹWhat did you ·say his ·name was?

6.3 asking for confirmation

6.3.1 of text
- **Did you say X?**
  Did you say anchovies?
- **Did you say X or Y?**
  Did you say dogs or docks?

6.3.2 of understanding
- **Do you mean to say +** *that*-clause?
  Do you mean to say that they aren't coming?

6.4 asking for definition or clarification
- **(Sorry) what does X mean?**
  What does anglophile mean?
- **What do you mean by X?**
  What do you mean by good?
- **What is X (exactly)?**
  What is kicking the bucket, exactly?
- **Could you explain that (for me, please)?**

6.5 asking someone to spell something
- **Could you spell that (word), please?**
- **How do you spell that (word), please?**

- How do/could you spell (spoken form), please?
  How do you spell [ruː bɑː b], please?

6.6 asking for something to be written down
- Could you write that down (for me), please?
- other request forms as in 3.3.5
  Do you mind writing that down for me, please?

6.7 expressing ignorance of the word or expression required
- I don't know how to say/ express it.
- I don't know what you call it.
- I don't know the word in English.
- In (native language) we say X.
  In German we say *Verdienstkreuz.*

6.8 appealing for assistance in finding an expression
- What is the English for (native language word)?
  What is the English for *funghi*?
- How do you say (native language word)?
  How do you say *hasta la vista* in English?
- use of hesitation fillers (see 6.9) with appropriate gesture

6.9 filling hesitation pauses while looking for a forgotten word or phrase
- ...er...
- ...you know...
- ...now let me think...
- ...just a moment...
- ...what's the word for it...
- ...how shall I put it...

6.10 substituting for a forgotten noun or name

6.10.1 using a meaningless noun or name
- ...what's-its/-his/-her name
  I met what's-his-name in town yesterday.
- ...what-do-you(-me)-call-it
  I need a what-do-you-call-it to fix this machine.
- ...thingummy(jig)
  I need a thingummy for opening a bottle.

6.10.2 paraphrasing
- a/some kind/sort of + generic term (+ specifier)
  We saw a kind of animal with a sort of long nose.
- something like + related term
  They grow something like a cabbage to eat.
- something/generic term + relative clause
  It's something you make with eggs.

6.11 asking someone to speak more slowly
- (Can/could you) speak (a little) more slowly, please.
- Not so fast/quickly, please.

6.12 what to do if the interlocutor does not understand

6.12.1 repeating what one has said
- X (simply repeated as originally spoken)
  I can't say I'm surprised.
- X (spoken more slowly and carefully)
  I cannot say that I am surprised.
- I said X
  I said seven hundred and thirty-five.

- **What I said was X**
  What I said was don't walk on the grass.
- **I said + indirect speech form or close paraphrase**
  I said I was very tired.
- **I told/asked you to + VPinf**
  I asked you to shut the door.
- **I asked you + indirect (*wh*) question**
  I asked you where the toilet was.

6.12.2 spelling out a word or expression
- **pronouncing the sequence of letter names**
  Rhubarb *R-H-U-B-A-R-B.*
- **X is spelt**
  Tough is spelt T-O-U-G-H.
- **You spell it**
  You spell it B-R-I-G-H-T.

6.12.3 correcting oneself
- **(Sorry) No, not X, Y!**
  No, not I want eating, I want to eat!

- **No, I mean(t) Y (not X)**
  No, I meant John, not Joan.
- **... or rather ...**
  I went there yesterday, or rather the day before yesterday.
- **That's not (exactly) what I meant.**
- **Let me try/start again.**

6.13 **asking if you have been understood**
- **Is that clear (now)?**
- **Do you understand (now)?**

6.14 **supplying a word or expression**
- **Do(n't) you mean X?**
  Do you mean mushroom?
- **Perhaps you mean X.**
  Perhaps you mean raspberry.
- **I think you (probably) mean X.**
  I think you probably mean a badge.
- **X perhaps.**
  An elephant, perhaps.

6 General notions

Introduction

The list of general notions is derived from a consideration of what, in general, people deal with by means of language, of what concepts they may be likely to refer to whatever the specific features of a particular communication situation may be.

We present the general notions under eight headings:

1 existential
2 spatial
3 temporal
4 quantitative
5 qualitative
6 mental
7 relational
8 deixis

The following list indicates the sub-classes of the notions selected and presents the various notions in the form of their exponents. Strictly speaking, we should have presented each notion and its exponent(s) separately, but since the large majority of the notions would then have to be referred to by means of the corresponding exponent – the lexical item *among* is the exponent of the notion *among* – this would have led to almost constant duplication without any practical gain.

General notions for *Vantage* including recommended exponents

1 Existential

1.1 *existence, non-existence*
There is + NP
There's no + NP
There isn't any + NP
verbs: to exist, to become, to make (as in: She made a new dress.), to create, to design, to produce; to destroy; to appear, to disappear

1.2 *presence, absence*
here, not here, there, not there, away; present, absent; presence, absence

1.3 *availability, non-availability*
to have (got)
There is (no) + NP
There isn't any + NP
available, not available; ready (as in: When will it be ready?)

1.4 *occurrence, non-occurrence*
to happen, to occur, to take place; event, occurrence

1.5 *discovery, non-discovery*
to find, to discover; to avoid, to miss; discovery

2 Spatial

2.1 *location*
noun: location, place, position, site, situation
adverbs: here, there, here and there, everywhere, somewhere, nowhere, (not) anywhere, where?, wherever; inside, outside; in the east/north/south/west
verbs: to be (as in: Harrods is in Knightsbridge.), to be situated, to lie
determiners: this, that, these, those

2.2 *relative position*
prepositions: above, against, among, at, at the end of, at the back of, at the side of, before, behind, below, beside, between, in front of, inside, in the centre of, next to, on, opposite, outside, over, round, under, with
where + sub-clause
adverbs and adverbial phrases: above, below, at the end, at the back, at the side, behind, in the background, in front, inside, in the middle, in the centre, opposite, outside
verbs: to cover, to overlap

2.3 *distance*
distance (as in: The distance from A to B is five miles.)
distant, far (away) (from), remote, near, in the neighbourhood (of), close (to), … away (as in: It is two miles away.)

2.4 *motion*
nouns: motion, movement
verbs: to arrive, to come, to come along, to come + to NP (as in: He came to the house.), to enter, to drop, to fall, to flow, to get up, to go, to hurry, to leave (as in: We have to leave now.), to lie down, to move (as in: The car did not move.), to pass (as in: You pass the railway station.), to quit, to remove, to roll, to run, to stand still, to start, to step, to stop, to walk

2.5 *direction*
direction (as in: In which direction is Slough?), destination
direct (as in: Is there a direct route to London from here?)
adverbs: away, back, backward(s), (anti-)clockwise, down (as in: Are you going down?), downward(s), forward(s), in, inward(s), out, outward(s), (to the) left/right, straight on, up, upward(s), east (as in: He went east.), north, south, west
prepositions: across, along, down, for (as in: He's leaving for Rome.), from, into, off, past, through, to, towards, up, away from
verbs: to bring, to carry, to follow, to pull, to push, to put (as in: May I put my coat here?), to send, to take (as in: I'll take it to your room.), to take away, to turn (as in: Turn left at the river.)

2.6 *origin*
from (as in: We came from London.), out of
origin, root(s)

2.7   *arrangement*
after (as in: B comes after A.),
before, between, among
first (as in: John came first.), last
arrangement, pattern, set

2.8   *dimension*

2.8.1   size
size (as in: What size shoes do
you take?)
adjectives: big, deep,
enormous, great, high, huge,
large, little, long, low, narrow,
shallow, short, small, tall,
thick, thin, tiny, wide
verbs: to become/get bigger,
smaller, etc., to increase, to
decrease, to grow, to shrink
nouns: depth, height, length,
size, thickness, width

2.8.2   length
length; centimetre, foot, inch,
kilometre, metre, mile,
millimetre, yard
long, short

2.8.3   pressure
heavy, light (as in: I want a light
blanket.), high, low
pressure
to press

2.8.4   weight
to weigh
load, weight
gram(me)s, kilo, lbs., oz.,
ton(ne)
light, heavy

2.8.5   volume
content; gallon, litre, pint
to contain

2.8.6   space
big, small
room (as in: You have plenty of
room here.), space

2.8.7   temperature
temperature, degree, zero (as
in: It's ten degrees below zero.),
heat, cold (as in: This cold is
bad.)
adjectives: chilly, cold, cool,
hot, lukewarm, mild, warm
verbs: to boil, to burn, to
freeze, to heat, to get
cold/hot/warm

3   Temporal

3.1   *points of time*
(three) o'clock, (five) to/past
(three), a quarter to/past
(three), (sixteen) minutes
to/past (three), half past
(three), (3) a.m./p.m., noon,
midnight, 1500 (fifteen
hundred), 1518 (fifteen
eighteen).
at . . .

3.2   *division of time*
moment, period, second,
minute, quarter of an hour,
half (an) hour, hour, day, week,
fortnight, month, year,
century; season, autumn,
spring, summer, winter;
afternoon, evening, morning,
night; weekend, holiday(s)
the names of days of the
week, names of months

3.3   *indications of time*
time (as in: What time is it?)
now, then, when?, whenever,
soon, ago (as in: two days ago)
today, tomorrow, yesterday,
the day after tomorrow, the
day before yesterday
this morning/afternoon/
evening/week/month/year,
tonight, last/next + week/
month/year
prepositions: at (as in: at three

o'clock), **by** (as in: by three o'clock), **in** (as in: in three days, in summer, in 1996), **on** (as in: on Thursday, on the twelfth of January)
dates: (spoken) the first of June, (written) 1 June. Christmas, Easter

3.4 *duration*
prepositions: **during, for** (as in: for three hours), **since, throughout, till, until, not ... till** (as in: He won't be here till three o'clock.)
verbs: **to continue, to go on, to last** (as in: It lasts three hours.), **to take** (as in: It takes three hours.)
adjectives: **long** (as in: a long time), **short, quick** (as in: a quick meal)
adverbs: **always, for good**

3.5 *earliness*
early (as in: You're early! There's an early train on Mondays.)

3.6 *lateness*
late (as in: We'll have to hurry, we are late. We were too late for the train. We went to the late show.)

3.7 *anteriority*
present perfect (as in: I haven't seen John yet. I've been to Paris.)
past perfect (as in: I hadn't done it.)
before + sub-clause
before (as in: I'd never done it before.)
already (as in: I have already done it.)
yet (as in: Has he come yet? He hasn't come yet.)
earlier than ...

3.8 *posteriority*
after + NP/sub-clause
afterwards, later (on)
later than ...

3.9 *sequence*
first (as in: First we went to Madrid.), **then** (as in: First we went to Madrid, then we travelled to Gibraltar.), **next** (as in: What did you do next?), **finally** (as in: Finally we went back.), **at last, later on, in the end, afterwards**

3.10 *simultaneousness*
when + sub-clause, while + sub-clause, as soon as + sub-clause, in the course of + NP, at the same time, in the meantime, meanwhile; instant(ly)

3.11 *future reference*
NP + be going to ...
NP + shall/will ...
present continuous of verbs of motion
simple present (with adverbials of future time) (as in: We leave at midnight.)
in (as in: in four weeks)
next week/month/year/ Sunday, etc., tonight, tomorrow, the day after tomorrow, this afternoon; immediately, soon, ultimately
future + N
the future

3.12 *present reference*
present continuous
simple present
present perfect
at present, now, today, still (as in: He is still working.); **this morning/afternoon/year**, etc.

3.13 *past reference*
past continuous
simple past
yesterday, the day before
yesterday, formerly, just, just
now, recent(ly), lately, of late,
last week/month, etc., in the
past, originally

3.14 *reference without time focus*
simple present (as in:
Edinburgh is in Scotland.)

3.15 *delay*
later (as in: The train will come
later.)
delay (as in: There will be a
delay.)
to be delayed

3.16 *speed*
speed
fast, rapid(ly), quick(ly),
slow(ly)
…miles/kilometres per hour

3.17 *frequency*
always, (hardly) ever,
frequent(ly), never,
occasional(ly), (not) often,
once, rarely, repeatedly,
seldom, sometimes, twice,
usually; daily, weekly,
monthly, annual(ly), hourly;
now and then; once every year
…times a/per week/month,
etc.
on weekdays/Sundays, etc.
every hour/week/Sunday, etc.

3.18 *continuity*
present continuous
past continuous
present perfect (as in: I've lived
here for two years.)
to continue, to go on

3.19 *intermittence*
not always, sometimes,
occasionally, on and off

3.20 *permanence*
always, for ever, for good,
permanent(ly)

3.21 *temporariness*
for + NP (as in: You can have my
car for a week.)
not always, temporary,
temporarily
present continuous
past continuous (as in: He
is/was living in Scotland for some
months.)

3.22 *repetitiousness*
again, again and again; all the
time, many times, several
times
to repeat

3.23 *uniqueness*
(only) once

3.24 *commencement*
to begin, to start (as in: The
game started at seven. He started
to speak.), to go (as in: Let's go
sailing.)
from (as in: I work from 9 to
12.), since (as in: I've been here
since 7 a.m.)
at first, initial(ly)
beginning, start (as in: at the
start of the season)

3.25 *cessation*
(to) end, (to) finish, (to) stop (as
in: The game will stop at six. He
stopped talking. It will come to a
stop soon.)
till, until, to (as in: from 9 to 12)

3.26 *stability*
to remain (as in: How long will
you remain here? Will it remain
dry today?), to stay (as in: I'll stay
here for a week. It won't stay dry
for long.), to keep (as in: How
long will this milk keep fresh?), to

wait (as in: We had to wait only five minutes.)

3.27 *change, transition*
to become (as in: Sugar has become expensive.), **(to) change, to get** (as in: He's getting old.), **to interrupt, to turn** (as in: The leaves turned yellow.), **to vary** suddenly...

4 Quantitative

4.1 *number*
singular/plural
cardinal numerals
ordinal numerals
fractions
minus, plus (as in: It is plus three degrees.), **negative, positive number**
to count
about (as in: I have about £25.), **approximately, exactly**
another (as in: May I have another cup of tea, please?)

4.2 *quantity*
determiners: **all, a lot of, any** (also: **hardly any, not any**), **both, each, enough, (a) few, (a) little, less, least, many, more, most, how much, how many, much, no, several, some, various**
double, twice, half (as in: Give me half of it. Give me the other half. Give me half a bottle.)
at least (as in: I need at least £5.)
extra, further, plenty (of)
per cent, sum, total, whole
to add, to subtract, to multiply, to divide
a bottle/box/cup/glass/ packet/piece, etc. of...
See further General Notions 2.8.

4.3 *degree*
comparative and superlative degrees of adjectives and adverbs
enough (as in: good enough), **too..., very...**
a bit (as in: a bit better; a bit tired), **a little** (as in: a little better; a little tired), **somewhat, a lot** (as in: a lot better), **much** (as in: much better), **almost, hardly, quite** (as in: quite old), **rather** (as in: rather old), **slightly** (as in: slightly better), **so** (as in: I'm so sorry.), **absolutely** (as in: It's absolutely wonderful.), **completely**
such (as in: It was such fun! He is such a nice boy!)
even (as in: I've even paid £5!)

5 Qualitative

5.1 *physical*

5.1.1 shape
adjectives: **circular, crooked, curved, oval, rectangular, round, square, straight**
nouns: **circle, curve, form, oval, rectangle, shape, square**

5.1.2 dimension
See General Notions 2.8.

5.1.3 moisture, humidity
damp, dry, humid, moist, wet
to dry, to (make) wet
humidity, moisture

5.1.4 visibility, sight
NP + can(not) see + NP
NP + can(not) be seen
to look (as in: Don't look now!), **to look at, to watch**
nouns: **look, glance, sight; darkness**
adjectives: **blind, (in)visible, dark, light**

5.1.5   audibility, hearing
NP + can(not) hear + NP
NP + can(not) be heard
to listen (to)
nouns: **noise, silence, sound**
adjectives: **deaf, loud, noisy,
silent, soft, quiet**

5.1.6   taste
to taste (of) (as in: How does
your soup taste? Would you like
to taste this? It tastes of garlic.)
flavour, taste (as in: I don't like
the taste.)
adjectives: **bad, excellent,
lovely, nice; bitter, salt(y), sour,
sweet**

5.1.7   smell
to smell (of) (as in: The food
smells good. Can you smell gas?
It smells of paint.)
smell (as in: The flower has a
nice smell.), **odour, perfume**
adjectives: **bad, nice, pleasant,
unpleasant**

5.1.8   texture
adjectives: **hard, rough,
smooth, soft, strong, weak**

5.1.9   colour
colour
adjectives: **blue, black, brown,
green, grey, orange, pink,
purple, red, white, yellow;
light** (as in: a light colour, light
blue), **bright, dull, dark** (as in: a
dark colour, dark blue)

5.1.10   age
age
I am ... (years old)
a(n) X-year-old boy/girl
How old are you (is he, she,
etc.)?
adjectives: **adult, elderly,
mature, middle-aged, old,
young**

nouns: **baby, child, adolescent,
teenager, adult; childhood,
adolescence, maturity, old age;
generation; week/month** (as
in: Her baby is six weeks/months
old.), **year**
**to be under/over age, to come
of age**

5.1.11   physical condition
verbs: **to break, to cut** (as in:
I've cut my finger.), **to (be) hurt,
to die, to fasten, to fix, to
recover, to repair, to put right,
to look** (as in: You look well.)
nouns: **death, health, life,
sickness**
adjectives: **alive, all right,
better** (as in: He got better.),
**dead, fine, ill, well
in/out of order** (as in: The
telephone is out of order.)

5.1.12   accessibility
verbs: **to close** (as in: The shop
closes at six.), **to enter, to get at,
to go in, to open, to reach**
adjectives: **closed, open**

5.1.13   cleanness
verbs: **to clean, to dust, to
polish, to wash**
adjectives: **clean, dirty, dusty,
neat, soiled**
nouns: **cleanness, dirt, mess**

5.1.14   material
nouns and adjectives: **cotton,
fur, linen, leather, nylon, silk,
wool(len); aluminium, brass,
brick, cardboard, concrete,
copper, glass, iron, metal,
paper, plastic, polyester, steel,
stone, wood(en); gold,
platinum, silver
material, textile(s)**

5.1.15 genuineness
false, genuine, imaginary,
imitation, real (as in: Is this real
leather?)

5.1.16 fullness
empty, full (of)
to empty, to fill

5.2 *evaluative*

5.2.1 value, price
How much + *be* ...?
(as in: How much are these
shoes?) to cost
nouns: price, value
adjectives: cheap,
(in)expensive, high, low,
valuable

5.2.2 quality
noun: quality
adjectives: bad, worse, worst,
excellent, fine, nice, perfect,
poor, pure, outstanding,
terrible, wonderful
verbs: to deteriorate, to
improve
adverbs: badly, excellently,
nicely, perfectly, poorly,
purely, outstandingly,
terribly, well (as in: He cannot
write English very well.),
wonderfully

5.2.3 rightness, wrongness
NP + should (not) + VPinf
NP + ought (not) to + VPinf
adjectives: right, wrong

5.2.4 acceptability,
non-acceptability
That's all right.
That's fine/nice.
It's just/not quite what I
wanted.
I don't like it.
I cannot accept ...
I'm against ...
satisfactory, unsatisfactory

5.2.5 adequacy, inadequacy
NP + *be* all right, fine, just
right
NP + *be* (not) enough
That will do.

5.2.6 desirability, undesirability
to like
See also Language Functions
2.5.16–2.5.23.

5.2.7 correctness, incorrectness
adjectives: better, (in)correct,
false, faulty, right, true, wrong,
OK
verbs: to be right, to be wrong,
to make something better, to
put something right, to
correct

5.2.8 successfulness,
unsuccessfulness
to fail, to succeed, to try
failure, success
(un)successful

5.2.9 utility, inutility
NP + can(not) use ...
helpful, practical, relevant,
(not) useful, useless

5.2.10 capacity, incapacity
NP + can(not) ...
NP + will/won't ...
NP + *be* (un)able to ...
to enable

5.2.11 importance, unimportance
(not) important, unimportant,
trivial

5.2.12 normality, abnormality
(ab)normal, strange, ordinary,
extraordinary, (un)usual,
unique

5.2.13 facility, difficulty
easy, difficult, hard (as in: His
English is hard to understand.)
ease, difficulty

5.2.14 discovery, non-discovery
to discover, to find; to avoid, to miss

5.2.15 complexity, simplicity
complex, complicated, simple
complexity, simplicity

5.2.16 convenience, inconvenience
convenient, inconvenient
convenience, inconvenience

5.2.17 generality, specificity
general, global; individual, particular, special, typical
to consist of
whole, part, detail, feature

6   Mental

6.1 *reflection, intuition*
verbs: to believe, to be sure, to be certain, to change one's mind, to conclude, to consider, to hope, to ignore, to imagine, to know, to neglect, to overlook, to remember, to take into account, to think, to wonder
nouns: belief, certainty, conclusion, hope, knowledge, opinion, thought, view
adverbs: naturally, no doubt, of course, on second thoughts

6.2 *expression*
verbs: to answer, to apologise, to ask, to command, to communicate, to discuss, to forbid, to invite, to laugh, to recommend, to refer(to), to relate, to remark, to remind, to report, to respond, to request, to say, to speak, to suggest, to talk, to tell, to thank, to write
nouns: answer, argument, communication, discussion, question, remark, report, statement, suggestion

7   Relational

7.1 *spatial relations*
See General Notions 2.2, 2.3, 2.5, 2.6, 2.7.

7.2 *temporal relations*
See General Notions 3.4–3.14.

7.3 *action/event relations*

7.3.1 agency
agent as subject
agent in by-adjunct
agent in emphatic It was I who ...

7.3.2 objective/factitive
objective as object (as in: John opened the door.)
objective as subject of passive (as in: The door was opened by John.)
factitive as object (as in: She made a new dress.)
factitive as subject of passive (as in: This cathedral was built in the thirteenth century.)

7.3.3 dative
dative as indirect object (as in: He gave me a book.)
dative in to-adjunct (as in: He gave the ticket to my brother.)
dative as subject of passive (as in: He was given a book.)

7.3.4 instrumental
instrumental in with-adjunct (as in: You can open the door with this key.)

7.3.5 benefactive
benefactive in for-adjunct (as in: I have bought this for my wife.)

7.3.6 causative
to have (as in: Can I have my shirt washed, please?), to make (as in: How can I make you understand?)

7.3.7 place
See General Notions section 2.

7.3.8 time
See General Notions section 3.

7.3.9 manner, means
in this manner, in this way,
like this, by means of,
somehow, thus; badly, fast,
hard (as in: We have to work
very hard.), how?, quickly,
slowly, well by + Ving
as (as in: They use it as a fork.)

7.4 *contrastive relations*

7.4.1 equality, inequality
(not) the same (thing) (as ...);
(dis)similar, different (from),
else (as in: Anything else?)
other, another (as in: Give me
another (= different) book.)
difference

7.4.2 correspondence
in addition to the exponents
of 7.4.1: like (as in: It's like an
orange.), unlike, equal (to)
comparative degree + than (as
in: John is older than his brother.
John works harder than his
brother.)
superlative degree (as in: He is
the tallest boy in the class.)
as ... as (as in: He is as big as his
brother.)
not so ... as (as in: He is not so
big as his brother.)
to compare

7.5 *possessive relations*

7.5.1 ownership, possession
possessive adjectives (my,
your, etc.)
possessive pronouns (mine,
yours, etc.) (as in: This is mine.
Mine is better.)

genitive singular of personal
nouns
of-adjuncts
with-adjuncts,
without-adjuncts (as in: You
cannot travel here without a
passport.)
to belong to ..., to have (got) (as
in: I've (got) a small car.), to get
(as in: I got a nice present from
him.), to give, to keep (as in:
May I keep this?), to obtain, to
own, to possess
owner
own (as in: This is my own book.)

7.6 *logical relations*

7.6.1 conjunction
and, as well as, both ... and,
also, too (as in: John is leaving,
too.), not ... either (as in: I
cannot swim either.), neither,
nor (as in: Nor can I swim.)
together
couple, pair (as in: I want to buy
a pair of shoes.), group (as in: a
group of friends)

7.6.2 disjunction
or, however, either ... or,
separate(ly), one by one, on the
other hand

7.6.3 inclusion, exclusion
with (as in: We are going to take
him with us.), without (as in:
We are not going without him.)
except (as in: We all went,
except John.)
(not) including, excluding
to exclude, to include, to omit

7.6.4 cause
cause
why ...?
because + sub-clause,
as + sub-clause
due to ..., because of ...

7.6.5 effect
  then ..., so ... (as in: He ate too
  much, so he did not feel well.), **so**
  ... that (as in: He ate so much
  that he fell ill.)
  the result is ...
  consequence
  consequently

7.6.6 reason
  why ...?
  because + sub-clause,
  since + sub-clause
  the reason is ...

7.6.7 purpose
  to ... (as in: He came to help
  me.), **in order to ... the**
  purpose is ...

7.6.8 condition, dependence
  if + sub-clause,
  unless + sub-clause

in case of, on condition that ...
to depend (on)
dependent (on), independent
(of)
dependence, independence

7.6.9 focusing
  about (as in: I don't want to talk
  about the war.), **on** (as in: I
  cannot give you any information
  on train services.), **as to,**
  concerning, as regards, with
  regard to
  only (as in: I only wanted to
  help.)

7.6.10 concession
  though, although, despite, in
  spite of, in fact

8   Deixis

Deixis involves referring or identifying by means of linguistic items belonging
to closed sets, the reference of which is dependent on the context of the
utterance (e.g. time, place, persons involved). Deixis may be definite or
indefinite (*he* vs. *someone*), non-anaphoric vs. anaphoric (i.e. referring to an item
already mentioned) (Why don't you come? vs. I'll buy those books because I need
them.).

8.1 *definite*

8.1.1 non-anaphoric
  personal pronouns (subject
  forms and object forms)
  possessive adjectives (**my,**
  your, etc.)
  possessive pronouns as
  complement (as in: This is
  mine.)
  possessive pronouns as
  subject (as in: Mine is better.)
  demonstrative adjectives and
  pronouns: **this, that, these,**
  those, such

  independent relative
  pronoun: **what** (as in: What
  you say is true.)
  definite article: **the**
  interrogative pronouns: **who,**
  whom, whose, what, which
  interrogative adjectives:
  whose, what, which

8.1.2 anaphoric
  personal pronouns (subject
  forms and object forms)
  possessive adjectives
  possessive pronouns as
  complement (as in: You take it,
  it's yours.)

demonstrative adjectives and pronouns
relative pronouns: **who, whose, whom, which, that,** omission of relative pronoun
reflexive/emphatic pronouns: **myself, yourself,** etc. (as in: I hurt myself. I've done it myself.)
reciprocal pronoun: **each other**
definite article: **the**
adverbs: **here, there, now, then, so** (as in: He wanted to go out, but he did not say so.)
propword: **one, ones** (as in: I like the red one.)
substitute verb: **do** (as in: He asked me to help him, and I did.)

8.2   *indefinite*
indefinite article: **an**
indefinite pronouns: **someone, somebody, no one, (not)... anybody, (not)... anyone, nobody, each, everybody, everyone,** **something, (not)... anything, nothing, everything, all** (as in: They all went home. I want all of it.), **both** (as in: They both went home. I want both of them.), **some** (as in: Some of them went home.), **it** (as in: It's raining.), **you** (as in: It is a nice record if you like modern music.)
indefinite determiners: See **General Notions, 4.2.**
adverbs: **somewhere, nowhere, (not)... anywhere, sometimes, never, always**
semi-deictics: **person** (as in: There are five persons present.), **man** (as in: There were animals here before man came.), **people** (as in: What do people think about the government? There are five people present.), **thing** (as in: What do you call that thing?), **do** (as in: What are you going to do tonight?)

7 Topic-related tasks and lexicon

Introductory

It is a basic characteristic of the model used in the description of *Waystage, Threshold* and the present objective that the linguistic apparatus required by the learners is derived from what the learners have to be able to do in and with the foreign language. In order to make this derivation possible in a systematic manner, the categories of *language functions* and *notions* were set up, language functions denoting in a general way what people do by means of language and notions indicating the concepts that people handle while using language. We furthermore distinguish *general notions* and *specific notions*. General notions are those which a learner may need to handle whatever the situational context in which a communication act may take place and are largely concerned with abstract, relational concepts, whilst specific notions are those which deal with more concrete details of the here-and-now. They are likely to occur particularly in certain situational contexts and, more specifically, in relation to certain transactions and certain topics.

The consideration of how the various language functions are performed and how the general notions are expressed provides us with the systematic core of the linguistic apparatus required. General notions are concerned particularly – though not exclusively – with its grammatical component, including closed lexical-grammatical categories such as prepositions and conjunctions. The specific notions form the basis for determining the more concrete vocabulary that the learners may have to be familiar with. Since, by definition, the specific notions are transaction-related and/or topic-related the ones particularly needed by the learners can only be determined once the transactions and topics concerned have been listed, together with indications as to what the learners are required to do with regard to each of them.

In the present chapter we are concerned with the selection of transactional situations and of topics, with the specification of what learners are supposed to be able to do with regard to each of them (the 'behavioural specification' or 'task descriptions') and with the conclusions that may be drawn from this with regard to the lexicon that may be required. We deal with these matters under the headings of *themes*, *tasks* and *lexicon* respectively.

Themes

Vantage is preceded by an earlier learning objective known as *Threshold*. Our description of *Threshold* has been based on our assumptions as to the situations which the members of our target group might be most likely to find themselves in and the things they might be most likely to need or to wish to be able to do in and with the foreign language in these situations, including the themes they would have to be able to deal with. It is a matter of course that if our assumptions made for *Threshold* have any validity they are also relevant to the same group of learners when they have reached a higher level of communicative ability. The consequence of this is that *Vantage* learners will be required to be able to do, among other things, that which was specified for *Threshold* with regard to each of the themes listed there. However, at *Vantage* level the learners will be expected to be able to do quite a lot more than at *Threshold* level. This will inevitably express itself in the quality of their overall performance, fluency, accuracy, grammatical skill, etc. (See also Chapter 14.) It does not mean, however, that they will necessarily need or wish to be able to do much more with regard to each theme or sub-theme listed in *Threshold 1990*. Not everyone will be interested in going as far as being able to give a report on a sports event or to engage in a discussion of public services. At the same time they may very well wish or need to be able to deal with quite different themes at a higher level than *Threshold* ability (e.g. banking, computers, film industry, religion). This means that in preparing for *Vantage* learners should be enabled to select, from within the *Threshold* list or from outside it, those themes to which, for their own purposes, they wish to give particular attention and with regard to which, ultimately, they may wish to give evidence of higher-level ability, for certification purposes or otherwise. To this extent, then, the learners will set their own individual objectives and, as far as this aspect is concerned, may have to take charge of part of their own learning. This is by no means utopian since the learning-to-learn components of earlier objectives – notably *Waystage* and *Threshold* – should have prepared them for the degree of learner independence required for this, and they will become increasingly skilled in this respect as their experience increases and their knowledge base expands.

In terms of the present objective the number of themes selected for higher-level treatment is less important than the depth and quality of the treatment. We can only say that the number should be large enough to ensure a certain spread of interests during the learning period and, if certification is desired, to guarantee an examiner that the learners' range of communicative ability is wide enough to justify an assessment in terms of general foreign language ability.

Tasks

For each theme in *Threshold 1990* the tasks are described which the learners are expected to be able to perform with regard to it. These 'behavioural specifications' involve:

- giving and obtaining information;
- expressing and exchanging views (notably opinions, likes, dislikes, preferences);
- describing simple events and occurrences;
- using services.

In addition to this, learners at *Vantage* level will, with regard to the topics chosen by them, be expected to be able to:

- express and account for their views, feelings and opinions;
- engage in discussions about them;
- describe/narrate complex events, occurrences, experiences and sequences of these;
- overcome problems which arise in the use of services.

Application of this extension to the themes listed in *Threshold 1990* would result in the following behavioural specifications at *Vantage* level.

1   Personal identification

The learners can describe themselves and others, stating names – with honorifics and titles as appropriate – and spelling them out if required, giving addresses and telephone numbers, date and place of birth, stating age, sex, marital status, religion, if any, and nationality; they can describe the composition of their family; they can say what they and others do or intend to do for a living – expressing their views and preferences on this and accounting for them if appropriate; they can state their likes and dislikes and account for them; they can describe and discuss the appearance, character and personality of other people; and they can elicit/understand similar information from others and discuss factual details, views and opinions as required.

2   House and home, environment

The learners can describe a house or flat and the rooms in it, refer to furniture, bedclothes and decoration, cost, services and amenities, describe regions, natural environment and geographical features, obtain/understand similar descriptions and references from others, exchange views on these matters, account for these views and discuss them with others. See also Chapter 3, section 1.2.

3 Daily life

The learners can describe their daily routines, at home and at work; can give information about income, schooling and prospects; obtain/understand similar information from others; exchange and discuss views on these matters. See also Chapter 3, sections 1.10 and 1.12.

4 Free time, entertainment

The learners can say when they are free and what they do in their spare time, particularly with reference to hobbies and interests, public entertainment and private pursuits, mass media, sports and reading; they can obtain/understand similar information from others; they can make full use of the relevant facilities; they can exchange views on these matters and account for and discuss their likes and dislikes; they can characterise and describe events and experiences, including the progress of sporting events and the contents of broadcasts, performances and reading matter. See also Chapter 3, section 1.8.

5 Travel

The learners can use and refer to means of transport by road, rail, sea and air for business and holiday purposes and use accommodation for travellers; they can describe journeys, exchange views on ways of travelling and types of accommodation, express their preferences and account for them, discussing them as required. See also Chapter 3, sections 1.2, 1.5, 1.6.

6 Relations with other people

The learners can refer to personal relations, participate in social life, deal with matters of correspondence, refer to club membership, refer to forms of government and politics, to matters of crime and justice, of war and peace, to social affairs; they can exchange information and views on these matters with others, engage in discussions and account for their views. See also Chapter 3, sections 1.13 and 2.

7 Health and body care

The learners can refer to matters of personal comfort, stating whether they feel well, are hungry, tired, etc., refer to matters of personal hygiene and obtain the articles required, refer to matters of health and illness and describe what is wrong to a doctor or dentist, report accidents, refer to medical services and insurance; exchange information and views on these matters; engage in discussion and account for their views. See also Chapter 3, section 1.9.4.

8   Education

The learners can exchange information and views on educational matters, particularly types of education, school subjects and qualifications; they can engage in discussions on these matters and account for their views. See also Chapter 3, section 1.10.

9   Shopping

The learners can use shopping facilities, particularly obtaining foodstuffs, clothes and household articles, discuss prices, pay for things bought; they can exchange information and views on these matters, engage in discussions on them and account for their views. See also Chapter 3, section 1.4.

10   Food and drink

The learners can refer to and order various kinds of food and beverage, also in a restaurant, café, etc.; they can exchange information and views on food, drink and places for eating and drinking; they can engage in discussions on these matters and account for their views. See also Chapter 3, section 1.3.

11   Services

The learners can refer to, enquire about, make use of and help others to make use of postal services, telephone, telegraph, bank, police, diplomatic services, car maintenance services and petrol stations. See also Chapter 3, sections 1.1.4, 1.7, 1.9.

12   Places

The learners can ask the way and give strangers directions; they can engage in discussions on where places are and how to get there. See also Chapter 3, sections 1.5 and 1.6.

13   Language

The learners can refer to foreign language ability and deal with problems of understanding, expression and correctness; they can exchange experiences and views on these matters, engage in discussions about them and account for their views.

14   Weather

The learners can understand and report a weather forecast and exchange information and views on climate and weather conditions; they can engage in discussions on these matters and account for their views.

For themes chosen by the learners outside the *Threshold* selection similar task descriptions may be drawn up using the indications at the beginning of the present section.

The additional requirements for *Vantage* marked the transition from *Threshold* to the present objective as a movement from the strictly personal and subjective to the more general interest and greater objectivity. If learners are to account for their views and discuss them with others this may involve:

- looking at their and others' views from a certain distance;
- analysing the issues involved;
- attempting a critical assessment of their own views and of alternative ones;
- weighing arguments;
- summarising the discussion;
- drawing conclusions;
- modifying or maintaining their point of view while supplying reasons for this.

The more complex forms of interaction involved make a greater demand on communication strategies than was the case at *Threshold* level. The additional requirement concerning 'describing/narrating complex events, etc.' will have more direct consequences for the command of discourse strategies needed by the learners.

Lexicon

Learners' progress after *Threshold* is marked by increasing individualisation and, consequently, divergence. While a common core may be distinguished in the development of their general foreign language ability (see, for instance Chapters 5 and 6 on language functions and general notions), their freedom to choose themes for higher-level treatment to suit their own interests rules out any attempt on our part to predict exactly what specific notions and what exponents may be particularly useful to them, beyond, of course, those already included in the *Threshold* specification.

What we can say with certainty is that, in order to carry out the tasks described for *Vantage* adequately, the learners will need to have a command of vocabulary that allows them to express themselves precisely and with some subtlety and to understand others doing so while being sensitive to shades of meaning, implications and overtones. This will imply a certain command of synonyms (different exponents for one and the same specific notion) and familiarity with situational (formal, informal, slang, etc.) and attitudinal (humorous, derogatory, etc.) features of vocabulary items. All this means that the learners' command of vocabulary will have to be much greater at *Vantage* level than it was at *Threshold* level. In fact, vocabulary extension may well constitute the greater part of the learning load required to pass from the earlier level to the present one.

We may give an indication of the scope of the vocabulary extension required by considering, for instance, the list of exponents recommended in *Threshold 1990* for theme 14, 'weather'. The list for this comparatively simple theme contains the following items only:

climate	fog	storm
weather	foggy	gale
sun	mist	thunderstorm
sunny	snow	snowstorm
sunshine	to snow	lightning
to shine	ice	fine
rain	frost	mild
rainy	to freeze	shade
to rain	wind	

In order to deal with this theme at *Vantage* level the following additional items will be by no means superfluous (and, please note that this list may be easily expanded, that it contains no items which are far-fetched, outlandish or in any other way unusual, and that most of them occur regularly in, for instance, the daily weather forecasts of the BBC):

moon	to thaw	muggy
star	breeze	close *(adj)*
planet	windy	humid
temperature	blustery	humidity
drizzle	severe (gale)	chill
to drizzle	hurricane	chilly
to pour (with rain)	blizzard	weather forecast
shower	thunder	low pressure
dense (fog)	bright	high pressure
visibility	cloud	anticyclone
snowflake	cloudy	isobar
hail	overcast	global warming
black ice	dull	ozone layer
frosty	unsettled	pollen count
thaw	murky	air pollution

Several further relevant items may be regarded as exponents of general notions, such as **hot**, **cold**, **dry**, **wet**, and, regrettably, **terrible**, **atrocious**, and even **diabolical**.

Note that the above list is here given as a quantitative indication. It is not suggested that learners should necessarily draw up such lists, or should be provided with them, for the themes chosen by them. Whether this may be considered useful or not is a matter of pedagogical views and individual learning habits.

Because the target group for *Vantage* is essentially the same as that for *Threshold* it is likely that many learners may wish to expand their communicative ability particularly with regard to certain themes of general interest that were included in *Threshold*. For their benefit we have added more advanced lists of lexical exponents for each of the *Threshold* themes and sub-themes as Appendix A. As noted before, it is likely, however, that learners may wish to be able to deal with other themes as well. It is, of course, not feasible to provide specific guidance for every conceivable additional or alternative theme. By way of exemplification we confine ourselves to the further presentation of one possible additional theme, namely that of 'religion'. In the *Threshold* list this occurs only as a sub-theme of 'personal identification' (theme 1.12). As a separate theme for *Vantage*, however, the requirements will be higher. The 'task' may be formulated as:

> The learners can refer to major religions and religious practices; they can engage in discussions on these matters and give their own views, accounting for them as may be required.

The specific lexicon required for this may at least contain the items listed under theme 1.12 in Appendix A. However, the degree of skill envisaged for a *Vantage* theme will make it necessary to consider also items such as the following:

(to) worship, worshipper	saint
to pray, prayer	heaven, hell
sermon	holy, sacred
mass, church service, ceremony	bible, gospel, testament, Koran,
altar	Talmud
churchyard	sect
cross	(to) sin
choir	pilgrim, pilgrimage
clergyman, imam	crusade, crusader
monk, monastery	Christmas, Easter, Whitsuntide
nun, convent	Church of England
prophet	Anglican
angel, devil	Presbyterian

8 Discourse structure and verbal exchange

The exponents of the functional categories given in Chapter 5 consist almost entirely of single sentences, phrases or words. Up to *Threshold* level, the focus has been placed on enabling the learner to participate effectively in oral interaction using short utterances so as to perform one function at a time, very often reacting to initiatives taken by a more experienced (e.g. native) speaker. Although in fact the resources available to the *Threshold* and even the *Waystage* learner enable longer contributions to be made, the psycholinguistic demands placed on a relatively inexperienced speaker make it advisable to break a conversation up into short turns.

At *Vantage* level, the learner may be expected to have greater control over linguistic resources and to be better able to call on them in order to organise more material into an utterance in real time, both by constructing sentences with a higher information value and by producing discourse in which a number of sentences are produced to form a coherent sequence. The principles by which this is accomplished therefore become of much greater importance than at earlier stages of learning.

Perhaps the simplest form of extension is to use the increased range of alternative exponents given in Chapter 5 in juxtaposition, as is common among native speakers. The effect is natural and, by increasing redundancy, enhances communication. For instance, in reply to Where is my box? The answer might be: Here. On the table, where you left it. (1.5.2.2). In reacting to bad temper (2.5.26), the learner may say Calm down! Don't get so worked up! There's nothing to get angry about. Expressing agreement (2.1.1.1) is further strengthened by sequencing: Yes, indeed. Well said. I quite agree. A sequence of comprehension signals (5.12) underlines the fact that they do not necessarily imply agreement. Really? Is that so? How very interesting.

The function for which longer turns are perhaps of greatest importance is 1.2, that of stating and reporting (describing, narrating), which involves the use of declarative sentences alone or, more commonly, in sequence. The function has an essential place at all levels. At *Waystage* level, learners will express themselves in very simple sentences and contribute to conversational and transactional exchanges by means of fixed formulae, short answers, simple noun phrases (i.e. determiner (+ adj.) + N (+ partitive)). Description and narration will, in most cases, consist of an extended string of simple sentences with little or no use of cohesive devices other than natural order and *and/but* linking. An acceptable account of something witnessed might be: '*I saw an accident. It was not very nice. It happened yesterday evening. A man was going on the road. He was very old. He had a long beard. It was white. It was dark and it was raining. He was in the road. He was pushing something. Some plastic bags were in it. His clothes were in them. A car came. The driver was driving too fast. He could not stop. The car hit the thing. The old man fell and broke his legs.*' This assumes, of course, that the learner had assimilated the *Waystage* resources well enough to recall the necessary vocabulary as required accurately and in proper order.

At *Threshold* level a much wider range of realisation is available for structural variables. In the case of the Noun Phrase, for example, not only is a much larger inventory of lexical nouns available, but also a range of adjuncts: adverbials, prepositional phrases (including partitive), *to* + infinitive Verb Phrases and relative clauses (cf. T-level Appendix B, B1). It is not, however, to be expected that a learner at this level will be able to use more than one or two of these at a time. It would then be possible for the accidents to be reported in some such terms as: '*I saw an accident yesterday evening in the High Street. It was horrible. There was a very old man with a long white beard. He was walking in the road and he was pushing a very dirty old pram. The pram was full of plastic bags. The man's clothes were in them. It was dark and raining, too. That is very dangerous. A car came too fast and could not stop. It hit the pram, so that the old man fell and broke his leg*', reducing the number of sentences from 17 to ten. Again, full meeting of the *Threshold* specification is shown, allowing the material to be organised more compactly and for some emotional reaction to be expressed.

At *Vantage* level the process is continued. In addition to an enriched vocabulary, the learner is able to use a wider range of constructions and combine them more flexibly, with greater use of cohesive devices and logical connections. The learner is also better able to integrate his/her intellectual and emotional attitudes to what is being said and towards the interlocutor. Thus the account can be differentiated between a formal report: '*At 10.15 yesterday evening, I witnessed an accident on the corner of the High Street and Chelmsford Road. Although it was dark and, in fact, raining, an elderly man was walking in the road, pushing a perambulator full of plastic bags containing his clothes and other possessions. Unfortunately, a car, travelling too fast, was unable to stop. It struck the perambulator, causing the man to fall and break a leg*', and an account given to a friend: '*I'd like to tell you about an accident I saw in the High Street yesterday evening. It was horrible. It came as a complete shock. There was this old man with a long white beard, pushing along a filthy old pram full of plastic bags with his clothes and other things in the road! I still can't believe it. After all, it was dark and actually raining! Anyway, just what you might expect happened. A car came along much too fast and couldn't stop. Unfortunately, it hit the pram and I'm afraid the old man fell down and broke his leg. Still, he wasn't killed. What a relief!'*

These examples show that an effective description or narration of events can be made at all levels. They also demonstrate some of the features of connected discourse which the learner is increasingly able to control as learning proceeds. It may be useful to look at some of these in greater detail.

Use of introductory adverbials

One functional development of the *Vantage* learner is the ability to indicate the status of what is asserted in a declarative sentence by the use of an introductory adverbial. This status may concern the attitude of the speaker towards his statement. Adverbials in this group are mainly derived from predicative adjectives in the frame: **I am being . . . when I say X**. The group includes: **frankly, honestly, bluntly, briefly, confidentially, personally, seriously, hopefully**. They can all be preceded or followed by **speaking** e.g. **Frankly speaking, . . .** or **Speaking personally, ...** Another group characterises the action or state expressed by the declarative sentence. These derive from predicative adjectives in the frame **It is/was . . . that X**. In this group are **(un)fortunately, naturally, undoubtedly, clearly, obviously, evidently, inevitably, strangely, essentially, (not) surprisingly, wisely, regrettably, arguably**. A small group is related to verbs of seeming e.g. **apparently, seemingly, presumably**. A further group defines the viewpoint of the speaker, e.g. **financially, politically, medically, educationally, theoretically, practically**. These can also be preceded or followed by **speaking** or paraphrased using an attributive adjective, e.g. in **from a financial point of view, ...** A group which is important for argument structure shows the logical relation of the following to the preceding sentence. This group, not generally derived from adjectives, includes: **actually, anyhow, also, anyway, besides, consequently, however, nevertheless, therefore, thus, hence, moreover, furthermore, still, otherwise, yet**, together with adverbial phrases such as **in fact, as a result, by the way**. For narrative cohesion, a *Vantage* learner will also be able to employ temporal adverbials such as **then, afterwards, later, meanwhile, earlier** (cf. Chapter 6, section 3).

The use of anaphora

More generally, in producing and understanding longer turns, a *Vantage* learner is aware and able to make use of various anaphoric means to refer to a referent previously identified.

- the use of pronouns, possessives, the pro-adverbials **there, then** and the pro-verb **_do_**
  - e.g. Juan comes from Andorra. *This* is a small country between France and Spain. *His* great grandparents lived *there* long before *he did*. Andorrans were mostly peasants *then*.

- the use of a superordinate generic noun for a more specific one
  - e.g. I saw a large fox. Before I could photograph *the animal*, it disappeared.

- the withdrawal of intonational prominence
  - e.g. You should give up smoking. Smoking can only harm you and harm you in more ways than one.

As content words, *smoking* and *harm* are prominent when first mentioned, but not subsequently.

Functional perspective

As we have seen, the important function of reporting (describing or narrating) has as its principal exponent (a sequence of) declarative sentences. An example of a declarative sentence might be An old man is walking slowly up a hill. As a piece of disembodied information, all the lexical words in this sentence: *old, man, walking, slowly, up* and *hill* represent new information. When the sentence is spoken, all these words will be stressed, and the intonational nucleus will be the last, but not necessarily the most important of these, namely *hill*. In the context of an actual communication, however, the information value of the ideas represented in a sentence is rarely equal. According to what is of importance for the speaker's intentions and what he or she believes the listener to know already, from general knowledge of the world, or of their common situation or of what has already passed between them, the ideas will have different weight and different functions in the utterance as a whole. For instance, it is common knowledge that people generally move about by walking. Accordingly, *walking* is not usually stressed, unless that particular way of moving is of particular significance. For example, in He walks to church every Sunday, *walks* will be stressed only if the distance is such that he would be expected to go by car. Again, since most people who go to church do so on Sunday, the intonational nucleus may appropriately be placed on *church*, since it is no longer to be expected of the general population, unless the regularity of the exercise is emphasised by placing the nucleus on *every* and leaving everything else non-prominent. The different possibilities for the distribution of stress in this sentence thus signal to the listener the functional significance of the different parts of the utterance. This appears most clearly when the sentence is produced in response to a question which identifies the focus of attention and indicates what can already be taken as given, e.g.

How does John keep so fit?	He *walks* to *church* every Sunday.
Where is John off to every weekend?	He walks to *church* every Sunday.
Is John a regular churchgoer?	He walks to church *every* Sunday.

The context given here by a question in a dialogue may also be given by preceding sentences in a longer turn, e.g.

Our organist is keeping himself fit these days.	He *walks* to church every Sunday.
I usually see John on the footpath at least once a week now.	He walks to *church* every *Sunday*.
John is now a regular churchgoer.	He walks to church *every Sunday*.

A contrastive focus can be placed on any word by the use of a high falling nucleus (for a final statement) or a falling-rising nucleus (in a non-final group). Thus in reply to the query: 'Can we have ·lamb ,chops ·on Tuesday? the answer might be: ˅Well, | ˅Frank ·eats ·meat, | but his ˅wife | is a veget˅arian.|| Here, *Frank* (fall-rise) is contrasted with *his wife* (fall-rise), and *vegetarian* (high fall) with *eats meat* (unstressed as already identified as topic by the question). The contrastive implication is so strong that the clause *but his wife is a vegetarian* becomes redundant and may be elided and left for the listener to reconstruct, or, if unable to do so, to query, e.g.
Can we have lamb chops on Tuesday?
˅Well, | ˅Frank ·eats ·meat.
ˋOh, | ˈdoesn't ,Mary?||
ˋNo. | She's a vegeˋtarian.

Clearly, the fact that one guest is a vegetarian is more significant for the discussion on what to cook than the fact that the other guest will be willing to eat the lamb chops. The English habit of using a fall-rise as a means of signalling a reservation which contrasts with and is more important than what is overtly said is a fruitful source of inter-ethnic misunderstanding. The *Vantage* learner should be aware of and able to recognise it, and to reconstruct or query the implications as necessary. Productive use, however, is only advisable if the interlocutor is seen to be able to deal with it.

While stress and intonation provide the speaker of English at *Vantage* level with an effective means of indicating focus and contrast, other syntactic devices are available. In the most straightforward case of a declarative sentence composed of a Noun Phrase followed by a Verb Phrase, the Noun Phrase establishes the topic upon which the Verb Phrase comments, the focus being on its final element. Thus in the train has left, *the train* is topicalised and *has left* provides information about it. In most cases, the subject NP, as topic, is given as part of the common mental context of speaker and listener (indicated in this case by the use of the definite article). In simple forms of discourse (e.g. the *Waystage* example given earlier in this chapter) there is a chaining process whereby the focal element in one sentence is topicalised in the following sentence, using one form or another of anaphoric reference, e.g. I saw an accident. It happened last night. The tendency to place new information into VP rather than the opening NP means that a sentence like: An old man is walking slowly up a hill is unusual as an opening sentence (except in literary writing). Rather, the 'existential' form There is an old man walking up the hill (which hill being contextually obvious) is preferred for the reporting of a state of affairs as opposed to a sequence of actions.

Other ways in which a particular element in a declarative sentence may be moved into focus are:

- **It was + focused element +** *that*-clause containing remaining elements (with intonational nucleus on the focused element)
  e.g. It was *Henry* that broke the blue vase. (= not *James*, etc.)
        It was the *blue vase* that Henry broke. (= not *the jug*, etc.)
        It was the *blue* vase that Henry broke. (= not *the green one*)

- **the + generic noun +** *that*-clause **+** *be* **+ focused element**. Again, the focused element carries the intonational nucleus.
  e.g. The person that broke the vase was *Henry*.
        The thing Henry broke was the *blue vase*.
        The thing Henry did was *break the blue vase*.
        The blue thing Henry broke was the *vase*.
        The vase Henry broke was the *blue one*.

Note that *the thing* may be replaced by *what*.

  e.g. What Henry did was *break the blue vase*.

These constructions are generally employed when the focused information gives the answer to a previously unresolved question, or corrects false information or a false belief. One of the introductory adverbials **(Oh) by the way, actually, as a matter of fact** is often used.

Verbal exchange strategies

As the *Vantage* learners' ability to understand and express reactions, intentions, emotions, etc. becomes deeper and more differentiated, the more flexible they become in their interactions with other speakers, and it becomes less and less useful to reduce verbal exchanges to set patterns. Instead, it becomes increasingly appropriate to frame objectives in terms of the interactional strategies and tactics language users may employ in different types of situation. For instance, the strategic aims of casual conversation among a circle of friends may be to develop friendship bonds by broadening and deepening the pool of common knowledge as well as the mutual understanding of the personalities, experiences, views, beliefs, intentions and feelings of the individuals concerned. Tactically, this strategic aim will be pursued through the selection of themes and the expression of opinions, intentions and feelings in respect to them as well as the observation, evaluation and memorising of the contributions of others. The interplay of statement, suggestion and agreement/disagreement, of question, answer and query, etc. all contribute to that process, which probably has a different significance for each of the participants. The objective of the learner is not to execute patterns of interaction, but to develop the friendship bonds in the ways shown, and the motivation for going beyond *Threshold* level is to improve the quality of the interaction by developing further the means for doing so and the control over the use of those means under the conditions and in the situations arising, which are only partially predictable or under the control of any one participant in a communicative interaction.

In the case of such casual conversations, the order of events is relatively free, beyond opening and closing routines. In goal-oriented co-operative transactions, the sequence of events is more closely determined. In the *Common European Framework of Reference for Languages: learning, teaching, assessment* (Cambridge: Cambridge University Press, in press) for instance, the following stages of such transactions are suggested.

- form the working group and establish relations among participants

- establish common knowledge of the relevant features of the current situation and arrive at a common reading

- identify what could and ought to be changed

- establish common agreement among the parties concerned on goals and on the action required to reach them

- agree roles in carrying out the action

- manage the practical actions involved, e.g. by
  - identifying and dealing with problems which arise
  - co-ordinating and sequencing contributions
  - mutual encouragement
  - recognising the achievement of sub-goals

- recognise the final achievement

- complete and terminate the transaction.

It is possible to identify the detailed functions, with exponents, that may be involved at each of these stages. Some may be simple, e.g. in Chapter 5, sections 3.8 and 2.5.5 give a range of expressions for encouragement. Others may involve lengthy and detailed negotiations in certain situations, yet be despatched in a few words in others. Some decisions may be self-evident or pre-determined and can be passed over in silence. Some participants may be taciturn and use language as little as possible, others loquacious, maintaining a continuous commentary on what is happening. Only in relatively routinised situations, such as buying and selling of goods and services, can relatively fixed schemata be set down, and the realisation of such schemata varies widely, as is demonstrated in Chapter 8 of *Threshold 1990*. Even then, the development of the learner between the *Threshold* and *Vantage* levels results principally in an enhanced ability to deal with predictable and unpredictable obstacles to the success of the transaction, e.g. by a more exact description of what is required, greater freedom to negotiate over price, quality, etc. and to recognise and deal with misunderstandings, etc.

The responsibility of any concerned with the learning process can only be to promote strategic and tactical awareness, to make the resources available to the learner for carrying them out and give opportunities to practise their application.

9 Dealing with texts: reading and listening

In relation to *Threshold*, *Vantage* is characterised by a relaxation of constraints. A major constraint at *Threshold* level is that the ability to deal with written and spoken texts that is expected of learners is related – and confined – to texts relevant to certain specified situations and to certain specified topics (see *Threshold 1990*, 3.3). At *Vantage* level the limitation to preselected situations and topics is abandoned (see also Chapter 7), and this means that, in principle, the understanding of texts relevant to any situation and to any topic may be required. Yet, *Vantage* is an objective for a particular target group – however large this group may be and however heterogeneous its composition – and it is still significantly lower than what is often referred to as 'near-native level'. Consequently, in describing communicative ability at *Vantage* level we have to provide criteria for the delimitation of the range of texts that learners may be expected to be able to deal with.[1]

These criteria are contained, explicitly or implicitly, in the following description of the relevant part of the objective:

The learner can understand the gist and relevant details, and identify the communicative intention, of written and of spoken texts which have the following characteristics:

1 they are directed at a readership/audience of average educational development;

2 they have a clear structure, both conceptually and formally;

3 the information contained in them is, on the whole, offered explicitly but may be implicit in transparent cases;

4 their understanding may require some familiarity with common features of the foreign culture;

5 they are produced in an easily accessible form:
   5.1 written texts are clearly printed or hand written and, when appropriate, provided with titles, paragraphing, illustrations, etc.
   5.2 spoken texts are produced with minimal acoustic distortion, in the standard pronunciation or a close approximation of this, and at a speech rate which is not above normal.

---

1 In this chapter we are not concerned with spoken texts in direct communication situations (face-to-face and telephone conversations with the learner as participant).

One aspect of the widening of the scope of the learners' ability to deal with texts, as compared with *Threshold*, is contained in the formulation that 'the learner can understand the gist *and* relevant details', where *Threshold 1990* has 'the gist *and/or* relevant details'. This means that at *Threshold* level the possibility of only partial understanding was admitted, related to the tasks that learners might be expected to be able to carry out with regard to a text, whereas at *Vantage* level more comprehensive understanding is expected. *Vantage* also has as a new aspect that learners are expected to be able to 'identify the communicative intention' of a text. We mean by this that the learners should be able to distinguish between:

1 texts primarily meant to provide factual information, such as (non-political) news items, interviews, announcements, etc.;

2 texts meant to influence the reader/listener, e.g. to get him/her to do something (to buy a certain product, to book a holiday trip, to vote for a certain political party, etc.), to form a certain opinion, to develop a certain view, to share a certain emotion, etc.;

3 texts primarily meant for amusement, entertainment.

Moreover, the learners should be aware of the possibility of occurrence of mixed forms of these three types of communicative intention.

The first of the text characteristics mentioned above concerns the level of cognitive and affective development that is expected of the members of the target group for *Vantage*. Obviously, the learners cannot be expected to be able to deal with texts that, even if they were translated into their native language, would be beyond their capacities of comprehension. If *Vantage* were designed as a foreign language learning objective for schools, there would be no problem because the expected stage of the learners' educational development would be given by the overall educational aims of the school type concerned and by the various subject-specific objectives collectively. However, *Vantage* is meant to be an independent language learning objective and this makes it necessary to indicate, at least in a general way, the overall level of development that may be expected of the learners. Now, among the kinds of text that learners will expect to be able to deal with at *Vantage* level are certainly news items and other texts of general interest as produced by the media. Although these texts may vary considerably in their degree of conceptual difficulty and in the 'knowledge of the world' presupposed by them, they usually have in common that they seek to address general audiences on a very large scale. We estimate that, on the whole, full understanding of such texts requires at least a developmental background corresponding to that of 15- to 16-year-olds in schools for general education in a European educational system or one similar to that. In the formulation of our first text characteristic we refer to this as 'average educational development'.

The second text characteristic means, basically, that the texts should be well constructed. This, as well as the third characteristic, may be considered as implied by the first.

For the fourth characteristic, see particularly Chapter 11 on sociocultural competence. Although in our discussion of the first text characteristic we suggested that at *Vantage* level the learners should be able to deal with texts which, if translated into their native language, would be understood by them, the demands made by a text on their sociocultural competence will often go beyond this. After all, most of the texts learners will wish to be able to understand will have been primarily written for native speakers and will presuppose familiarity with common features of their culture.

The first part of the fifth characteristic (5.1) simply reflects what will be the normal condition of texts met by the learners in natural circumstances, with the possible exception of handwritten texts. In test conditions, of course, the quality of handwriting should be such that it causes no problems. The specification under 5.2 imposes more significant limitations on what learners may be expected to understand. Even near-natives usually score significantly lower in respect of tolerance of deviations on each of these points than native speakers do. At *Vantage* level, we feel, one cannot reasonably expect more of learners than what is stipulated here. The formulation 'in the standard pronunciation or a close approximation of this' requires further elucidation. If by 'standard pronunciation' we refer to the pronunciation of educated speakers from the southeast of England, we have to recognise the fact that, even if we exclude non-native speakers, the large majority of speakers of English have pronunciation habits that deviate from this 'standard', and often very considerably. In fact, the range of deviations is so great that learners cannot be expected to be able to cope with all of them. Hence our formulation 'or a close approximation'. We mean by this the range of deviation as exhibited by the various announcers and interviewers employed by the BBC for nation-wide broadcasts. These speakers use either the standard pronunciation or what might be referred to as 'standard regional'. These various accents are supposed to be understood by speakers of English generally and learners at *Vantage* level may expect to be able to cope with them as well.

No indications are given as to the range and nature of the grammatical and lexical content of the texts to be understood. At *Vantage* level learners should be familiar with the basic grammar of the foreign language so that no limitations need to be put on the range of grammatical structures that they should be able to cope with in text interpretation. Yet, through multiple embedding and concatenation basically simple structures may be developed into highly complex ones. Extremes in this respect may still be beyond the learners' comprehension. The degree of complexity admissible in texts for *Vantage* may be considered an aspect of conceptual difficulty and is thus implied in the first text characteristic mentioned above. The same characteristic may also serve as a rough indication of the lexicon that learners at *Vantage* level may be expected to be able to cope with. However, at this level this 'coping' will often require opportunities for reflection, for the application of relevant compensation strategies (see Chapter 12), and particularly for the consultation of a suitable dictionary. In normal conditions such opportunities usually exist when the learners are dealing with written texts (exceptions are subtitles of films and TV programmes, and road signs). With spoken texts the situation is very different. In normal circumstances they are produced only once and in a linear form, which does not allow the listener to go back to earlier parts or to reflect on the text as a whole as easily as may be done with written texts. The inevitably restricted lexicon of learners at this level may then be insufficient to achieve full understanding instantly. However, if the learners have developed adequate skill in the application of interpretation strategies and compensation strategies, they should, even if after some delay, be able to understand at least the gist and much of the relevant detail, particularly if the texts involved contain sufficient redundancy. Conditions are more favourable to the learners, of course, if they have recorded texts at their disposal with opportunities for repeated listening.

Some text types, however, are likely to cause particularly great difficulties, and, although some degree of understanding is not to be excluded, they remain outside the scope of the ability to be expected of the learners. Even though texts belonging to these types may be meant for a general public, they do not, as a rule, satisfy all the criteria involved in our list of text characteristics. These text types include those represented in:

- drama performances

- film dialogues

- soap operas

- comedians' performances

- sports commentaries

Very often texts belonging to these types do not satisfy our criteria on one or more of the following points:

- conceptual difficulty

- acoustic distortion

- deviation from standard pronunciation

- rate of delivery.

In *Threshold 1990* we listed those text types that we felt to be particularly relevant in the framework of that objective. In view of the 'relaxation of constraints', which marks *Vantage*, we refrain from giving similar lists in the present volume. At this level the still existing limitations in the learners' ability are not primarily to be found in the exclusion of particular text types but in the extent to which individual texts exhibit particular text characteristics. As we pointed out above, this criterion will almost automatically exclude certain text types. However, this is not because these text types are unsuitable in themselves but because very often texts falling within these types do not exhibit the whole range of the characteristics listed by us.

It is a matter of course that, at this level too, the learners will be able to benefit considerably by skill in the use of various interpretation strategies. As we noted above, such skill may even be indispensable if they are to cope with certain oral texts. The strategies listed in *Threshold 1990* (Chapter 9) remain valid for *Vantage* as well:

- distinguishing main points and secondary points

- distinguishing fact from comment

- identifying relevant information

- making use of clues such as titles, illustrations, typography (e.g. bolding, italics, capitals), paragraphing, and, in oral texts, discourse markers such as phrasing, the placing of emphasis, structurally relevant pauses, tone of voice, etc.

There are further techniques that may be usefully employed towards achieving understanding of a text. These techniques, which include segmentation, the establishment of links between segments, underlining, note-taking and note-making, etc., may be profitably practised in a learning programme designed to enable learners to arrive at the required text comprehension, but they are not presented as components of the objective itself because the extent to which each individual learner makes use of them in satisfying the requirements of the objective is subject to personal variation. In the same way, such strategies as inferencing, hypothesising from proper names, international words, cognate words in the learner's mother tongue or in other languages he or she may have learnt, are all too variable to be specified in a general performance objective. However, an awareness of such techniques and strategies, and experience in their use, form an important aspect of learning to learn (see Chapter 13).

10 Writing

The learners can perform, within the limits of the resources available to them at *Vantage* level, those writing tasks which adult citizens in general may wish, or be called upon, to carry out in their private capacity or as members of the general public.

Such tasks are of the following kinds:

• completing forms;

• writing letters:
  - formal letters
  - informal letters (including short messages conveying information as well as greetings and congratulations);

• making notes, summaries, etc.

On the whole, the completion of those 'forms' that the learners are most likely to have to be able to deal with requires more reading ability than skill in writing the foreign language. Hotel registration forms, membership application forms, subscription forms, etc. demand little more than the ability to write one's own name and address, to write dates (figures usually suffice), to tick boxes, to write the words *yes* and *no*, and perhaps to supply some further personal information well within the scope of learners at lower levels than *Vantage*. Of a more demanding nature, however, are such forms as are in use for reporting accidents, claiming damages, etc.

'Formal letters' include those referred to as 'standard letters' in *Threshold 1990* (p. 92):

• enquiring about price and conditions of accommodation

• stating wishes as to size of rooms, arrangement (full board, etc.), amenities, view

• enquiring about tourist attractions, sights, etc.

• booking accommodation.

At *Vantage* level the learners' ability is no longer confined to such standard letters. They should be able to write all those kinds of letters that, also as temporary residents in an English-speaking country, they may wish or need to write in their private capacity, e.g. letters to authorities, companies, service departments, shops, businesses, with enquiries, requests, complaints, proposals, confirmations, reports on accidents, insurance claims, etc.

'Informal letters' are particularly letters to those relatives, friends and acquaintances with whom they communicate in the foreign language and may be about anything of interest to the learners themselves and, presumably, to the addressee. In conformity with the relaxation of constraints characterising *Vantage* there are no limitations as to topic or nature of treatment. Learners should simply be able to write about such matters and in such a way as they need or wish to do, even though they may still do this in a fairly simple way.

In writing letters – both formal and informal – the learners should be able to observe current conventions regarding:

- differences between more formal and more informal language
- basic letter layout
- appropriate opening and closing formulae (cf. 5.5.21.1–2)
- representation of dates (cf. 6.3.3)
- use of capitals and punctuation.

Learners who can write letters of the types referred to above will, on the whole, have little difficulty in carrying out tasks such as the making of notes and summaries. If these are for their own use, of course, they can always have recourse to their native language. However, at *Vantage* level learners may also expect to be able to carry out such tasks for the benefit of others, including speakers of the foreign language.

11 Sociocultural competence

Sociocultural competence is that aspect of communicative ability which involves those specific features of a society and its culture which are manifest in the communicative behaviour of the members of this society. These features may be classified as 'universal experiences', 'social rituals' and 'social conventions' (see below). The degree of familiarity with them which is required for successful communication depends on the circumstances in which the communication takes place. It will probably be higher in contacts with native speakers of the foreign language (especially when the learner is a temporary resident rather than a visitor) than when the foreign language is used as a *lingua franca*. Like *Threshold*, *Vantage* is designed to suit all these types of contact. This means, on the one hand, that in attempting to indicate what may be expected of a learner at this level we have to focus on the more predictable kind of contact, that with native speakers of the foreign language and particularly with such native speakers in their own country. On the other hand it means that an alertness has to be stimulated in the learners to unexpected sociocultural differences between their communication partners and themselves. This applies particularly when English is in use as a medium of international communication between non-native speakers from different cultures. Learners cannot take it for granted that their interlocutor will share either their own values, attitudes, beliefs and social conventions or those of Anglo-Saxon peoples. They will need to be alert to signs of cultural differences, to be tolerant of such differences, and to be prepared to operate whatever strategies may be needed to establish a proper base for communication by raising cultural differences into consciousness. This presupposes a certain degree of self-awareness and the ability to articulate one's own cultural distinctiveness.

If alertness to sociocultural differences is a general requirement for effective and efficient communicative interaction with native speakers of other languages – as it was, indeed, specified for *Threshold* as well – *Vantage* presupposes a much more thorough familiarity with common sociocultural features of at least one of the major English-speaking communities of the world. At this level mere 'alertness to differences' will not suffice in order to meet the requirements for the various skills dealt with elsewhere in this document, particularly reading and listening. The understanding of even the gist of newspaper articles and broadcasts of a general character may require a degree of familiarity with the foreign culture involved that is unlikely to be reached without deliberate attention having been paid to this culture and to its major internal varieties.

And even if such study has been part of the students' preparation for *Vantage* there may always remain matters that can hardly be intelligible to someone who has not been a resident in the foreign country for a considerable period.

A particular problem in the case of the English language – as it is for some other 'world languages' – is that there is not one single sociocultural context in which it is used as a native language, but that there are several. The sociocultural contexts in which American English, Australian English, British English, South African English and many other 'Englishes' are used differ considerably in many of their distinctive features, and learners, even at much higher levels than *Vantage*, cannot be expected to be familiar with all of them. In the present study we follow European educational tradition by requiring the learners primarily to be familiar with British English in its own sociocultural context. This is justifiable not only on the grounds of tradition and common practice but also because British English is the common root of all the other varieties, and is therefore likely to share more common features with each of them separately than any of the latter with all the others. In other words, we assume that familiarity with British English and its sociocultural context provides a suitable basis for the exploration of other varieties wherever they may be found in the world.

A detailed specification of just what people have to know about a particular sociocultural context in order to function satisfactorily in it is obviously impossible for a target group as heterogeneous as that for *Vantage*. Just what people 'need to know' depends very much on their own individual interests and backgrounds and the types of contacts they are likely to have. All we can do here is to list a number of broad areas that learners will find it necessary to have a certain degree of familiarity with. The height of this degree of familiarity will vary from one individual to another and it is particularly important, in this respect, that the learners should know how to increase their sociocultural competence whenever they feel the need for this. Any attempt to be more specific would involve choices of such an arbitrary nature that their validity would be unacceptably low.

Sociocultural competence for English at *Vantage* level

I   ## Universal experiences

Learners are aware of the major differences between their own culture and that/those of the British Isles and sensitive to the diversity of other cultures in respect of:

1 everyday life

- at what times people have their regular meals and in what ways the composition of meals, including beverages, typically differs from that in their own country;
- major national holidays;
- working hours;
- preferred leisure activities (to the extent that generalisation is possible);
- normal patterns of domestic routine.

2 living conditions

- living standards in relation to income, accommodation, education, social welfare, etc., including significant differences between social classes and major parts of a country, particularly Britain;
- ethnic composition of the population.

3 interpersonal relations

- class structure of society and relations between the classes;
- relations within the family and between generations;
- formality/informality in work situations and in contacts with officials;
- interracial relations;
- major political groups.

4 major values and attitudes

i.e. the value generally attached to and the prevalent attitudes towards:

- social class;
- wealth and security;
- tradition;
- national identity and foreigners;
- politics and social affairs;
- religion.

II Social conventions and rituals

1 non-linguistic

a) body language

The learner is aware of the diversity of conventions in different countries with regard to hand shaking, touching, embracing, kissing, gesticulation, close physical proximity and protracted direct eye contact and is able to avoid the embarrassment that may be caused by non-observance of the conventions followed by the interlocutor. He/She is familiar with the conventions generally adhered to in Britain.

b) visiting rituals

As visitors, the learners know – or can enquire:

- within what limits they are expected to be punctual;
- whether they are expected to bring a present, and if so what sort of present;
- what sort of clothes are appropriate to different occasions;
- whether to expect refreshments, or a meal, if asked for a certain time or for a particular occasion;
- whether, and how, they are expected to comment on food, furnishings, etc.;
- how long they are expected to stay as well as when and how to take leave.

As hosts, they are aware of the need to make their own expectations clear to visitors from other countries.

c) eating and drinking rituals

The learners are aware that rituals may differ from what is customary in their own country, and are ready to observe, and, if appropriate, follow others' examples. They are familiar with the rituals generally current in Britain.

2   linguistic

The learner is aware of the sociocultural conventions governing the use of the language functions listed in Chapter 5 of this document, and can perform them appropriately. He/She is aware of the conventions of politeness described below and is able to act appropriately in this respect.

III   Politeness conventions

The exponents of functional and notional categories recommended for use by foreign learners are, in general, of a relatively simple and direct character. This is particularly the case for *Waystage* and, though to a somewhat lesser extent, *Threshold*, where the learning emphasis is placed on the minimal resources needed to deal in a fairly straightforward way with the requirements of transactions and personal interaction in as wide a range of social situations as possible. If learners use the foreign language in this way it is likely that their interlocutors, too, will use language to communicate with them in a simpler and more direct fashion than they would do in conversing, say, with friends sharing the same mother tongue and social background.

The increased resources available to *Vantage* learners and their greater control over them make it possible for them to go beyond this relatively simple and direct way of using the foreign language. As they progress beyond *Threshold* they will become increasingly familiar with more complex and less direct kinds of usage in the target language. They will observe the differences in the language used by native speakers according to the nature of the situation and the relations between speakers, ranging from the familiar to the formal. They will be better able to select varieties of usage appropriate to their age, sex, social class, role and personality type, so as to act in a coherent way whilst adjusting to the requirements of the situation and their relation to the conversation partner(s). Unless there are powerful reasons for them to identify with a particular social group, they will probably wish to adopt 'unmarked' options, avoiding the extremes of familiarity and formality as well as strongly marked class or generation markers. Like most English speakers they will be aware of colourful idioms and expletives but be extremely cautious in their use, certainly until such time as their sociocultural connotations are fully understood! In general, *Vantage* learners will depart from straightforward usage only when they have reason to believe it appropriate to do so (e.g. polite, hyperbolic, ironic, euphemistic, imaginative and ludic usage) and when they are reasonably confident that their partner will understand this 'indirect' usage.

Of these indirect uses of language, the most important for learners to understand and where possible conform to, are the conventions of *politeness*. Whilst they are based on some universal considerations, such as showing respect and concern for the partner, they take different forms in different communities and it is possible for the foreign learner who is unaware of the conventions to be misinterpreted and give unintentional offence to partners who are themselves unaware that the conventions they follow are not shared by the whole world. Many foreigners try to compensate in this respect by smiling, making eye contact and generally showing goodwill through body language. Unfortunately, the conventions of body language also vary considerably from one culture to another and smiles and eye contact can be misunderstood as intrusive in one and their absence misunderstood as rejection in another. It is therefore increasingly important for learners, particularly as their linguistic and pragmatic command of a language improves and arouses higher expectations in their interlocutors, to be aware of the main features of politeness in speech so as to recognise them in the speech of others and respond appropriately. Such awareness is probably as far as *Threshold* learners are likely to progress. *Vantage* learners will have acquired greater familiarity and be more confident in following the same principles in their own speech, insofar as they feel them to be appropriate to the situation, their relation to the partner and their own sense of identity. They will be aware of the dangers of appearing timid or obsequious through the excessive use of polite formulae on the one hand, but also of the dangers of appearing rude or arrogant by seeming insensitive to the partner's feelings and interests. Sociocultural awareness should produce an enriched 'intercultural' personality, developing in a coherent way so as to be able to interact flexibly and sensitively with a widening range of persons, situations and cultures. Each learner will find a unique resolution to the pressures of influences which may pull in different directions. The analysis of English politeness conventions which follows should not therefore be regarded as prescriptive, mandatory upon all learners of English, but rather as providing useful guidelines in dealing with those English speakers who follow these conventions or some variant of them. It may also serve to raise awareness of indirect language usage more generally.

The twin principles of concern and respect for the partner lead to two kinds of politeness: positive and negative. 'Positive' politeness is shown by expressing interest in partners' interests, activities, opinions, beliefs, etc., congratulating them on their achievements, praising their qualities, etc., but also sympathising with their troubles and sharing one's own. It may go together with physical closeness and contact, prolonged eye contact and sharing of emotional signals. Positive politeness contrasts with 'negative' politeness, in which the speaker tries to avoid embarrassment, distress or displeasure by showing an awareness of the demands made on the partner by what the speaker says. In this way the possibility of overt conflict with possible hurt or offence is avoided or at least reduced. Politeness conventions in British English are particularly of this kind. They can be embodied in a number of maxims:

1 *Do not be dogmatic.* Remember that the partner may have a different opinion. This maxim applies to the functions of imparting factual information and expressing attitudes. It implies qualifying simple declarative sentences in the following ways:

   a) the use of *I think, I believe, I expect,* as introducers or as tags. If they are unstressed, their use does not indicate uncertainty or lack of confidence;
      I think his mother is Italian. She comes from Calabria, I believe.

   b) the use of *you know, of course,* to imply that the partner is not ignorant;

Of course, his mother is Italian, you know.

c) the use of tag questions to invite the partner's agreement (falling intonation) or confirmation (rising intonation).
His 'mother is I'talian, `isn't she? (inviting agreement; no uncertainty);
His 'mother is I'talian, ‚isn't she? (asking confirmation; uncertain).

Correcting is liable to give offence, since it involves telling the partner that he/she has made a mistake. Offence can be avoided by:

a) apologising for correcting;
I'm sorry, but the lecture isn't on Wednesday. It's on Friday.

b) querying what has been said, so that the partner can correct the slip;
Blue? Did you say her dress was blue?

c) presenting the correction as a different opinion;
Fifty-four? I thought eight sevens were fifty-six.

d) requesting confirmation by the use of a question tag.
Nicaragua? San Jose is in Costa Rica, isn't it?

2 *Be reluctant to say what may distress or displease the partner.* This applies to such functions as breaking bad news, expressing disagreement, declining offers and invitations, saying that the partner is obliged to do something, prohibiting and withholding permission, expressing displeasure, dislike, dissatisfaction, disappointment and disapproval. The maxim implies such strategies as:

a) expressing reluctance;

I don't want to complain but . . .	(e.g. this soup is cold).
I don't want to be difficult but . . .	(e.g. this machine doesn't work).
I don't like saying so, but . . .	(e.g. the music is too loud).

b) seeking the partner's agreement;

I hope you don't mind my saying so, but . . .	(e.g. those colours don't mix).
Don't you agree that . . .?	(e.g. that colour is rather too bright).

c) apologising or expressing regret
I'm sorry, but your work is not good enough.
I'm afraid you haven't passed your exam.

This is especially frequent in prohibitions and withholding permission.
I'm sorry, but you can't leave tomorrow.
I'm afraid you can't smoke in here.

d) using euphemisms

Your work isn't very good . . .	(= your work is bad).
I can't say I like it . . .	(= I dislike it).

e) implying something unpleasant rather than stating it openly.
   I'd like to help you . . .   (implying 'but I can't').
   Your ideas are interesting . . .   (implying 'but I don't agree
                                                  with them').

Note that frequent use is made of falling-rising intonations in these cases.

Expressing disagreement is likely to cause offence and to lead to conflict. The risk can be reduced by:

a) apologising for not agreeing.
   I'm sorry, but I don't agree.

b) expressing regret for not agreeing.
   I'm afraid that isn't true.

3 *Do not force the partner to act.* Allow him/her to appear to act voluntarily. This maxim applies to the functions of suasion, seeking factual information and finding out attitudes. It implies:

a) adding *please* when you call for action by the partner;
   Where is the toilet, please?   (asking for information)
   A return ticket to London, please.   (requesting something)
   Sit down, please.   (giving instructions, orders)

b) avoiding simple imperatives when asking the partner to do something for you. Instead
   i)   ask if he/she
        is willing to act
        Will you open the window, please?
        is able to act
        Can you open this tin for me, please?
        wishes to act
        Would you like to help me, please?
   ii) use introducers such as
        I wonder if . . .
        I wonder if you could close the window, please?
        Do you think . . .
        Do you think you could open this tin for me, please?
   iii) use warnings or advice
        Don't forget to post the letter.
        If I were you, I'd keep your eyes on the road.
   iv) draw attention to the situation, inviting the partner to recognise that there is a problem that needs to be dealt with
        It's cold in here, isn't it? (= Please close the window.)
        I can't open this tin. (= Please open it for me.)
        Dinner's ready. (= Come and sit down to eat it.)

Asking is a form of suasion, since the partner is asked to do something for you, namely provide information. *Wh* questions are normally accompanied by 'please'. After the partner has replied it is normal to thank him/her for doing so.

What's the time, please?
Twelve o'clock.
Thank you.

Offers and invitations are very much subject to politeness conventions, but in a complex way, since they attempt to persuade the partner to act in a certain way, but in the interests of the partner rather than of the speaker. Invitations and offers may be strong or weak.

A 'strong' offer or invitation, making it easier for the partner to accept, may be conveyed:

a) by using an imperative, as though it were an order
    Let me help you.
    Give me that case to carry.
    Come and spend the day in Oxford.

b) by expressing obligation or necessity, as though the partner had no choice
    You must let me carry that case.

c) by demanding a promise
    Promise you will come to dinner with us.

d) by demanding confirmation of an imputed intention
    You will be our guests, won't you?

Note that the use of low falling intonations is normal with strong offers and invitations.

A 'weak' offer or invitation makes it possible for the partner to decline by using an interrogative question regarding the partner's intentions, desires, needs or ability.

Are you coming to dinner?
Would you like some help with that problem?
Do you need any help?
Can you come to dinner next Wednesday?

Especially weak are offers that;

a) require the partner to admit that he/she is unable to refuse;
    Can you manage?
    Are you stuck?

b) are negatively phrased.

> I don't suppose you could do with some help?
> You don't require assistance, do you?

Note that a rising intonation is used with weak offers.

Strong offers can be accepted without demur, or confirmation can be invited:

> Are you sure?
> Is that all right?

A weak offer or invitation is not usually accepted without demur. More commonly, a repeated offer is invited:

> Won't that be too much trouble?
> Can you really spare the time?
> It's very heavy, that case.

or a weak rejection is offered:

> No, thank you, I don't want to bother you.
> I'm sure you're much too busy.

This allows the partner to withdraw the offer or invitation:

> Well, as a matter of fact, I am rather busy.
> Right then. So long as you can manage.

or to repeat it, usually in a stronger form:

> No, really. I'd like to help.
> No, do come. We'd very much like you to come.

The declining of a strong invitation is usually accompanied by an apology, or a reason for declining an offer:

> Well, thank you, but I'm sorry, I'm afraid I have another engagement.
> No thank you, I don't smoke.
> Thanks, but it's easier by myself.

A suggestion for further contact, or even an invitation to visit, may be a polite or a well-intentioned way of ending a contact. Its formal acceptance need not entail a firm commitment on either side:

> **A:** Do visit us next time you're in London.
> **B:** Thank you, I will.

Apologies are often called for in social life, for reasons ranging from the trivial and conventional to serious damage or inconvenience. For brushing against someone in passing perfunctory apology is sufficient:

> Sorry.

On the other hand, if damage or inconvenience are caused, as when you keep someone waiting for an appreciable time, the apology normally involves an explanation:

> I'm very sorry to be so late. I'm afraid I missed the train.

The politeness conventions described above are widely used and understood in English-speaking countries, especially between speakers in the roles appropriate to foreign learners up to *Vantage*. Learners at *Vantage* level should be able to recognise their use and to identify the attitudes and intentions of speakers who use them. They should also be able to use them appropriately themselves, bearing in mind that their use is governed by such factors as:

- the social and regional groups to which the speaker belongs. There are differences in usage between men and women, working and middle class, the North and South of Britain, etc.;
- the speaker's personality: some people are more direct, others more sensitive to the feelings of other people;
- the relations of the conversational partners: close friends need make less use of politeness conventions than acquaintances or strangers;
- the nature of the situation: urgent emergencies demand immediate decisive action. Where conflicts of interest arise and polite methods fail, a learner may well need to be frank, even blunt in speaking his/her mind.

12 Compensation strategies

No matter how hard we try to assess and to predict learners' communication needs, to determine the situations requiring foreign language use which they are most likely to find themselves in, and to help the learners to identify those language forms which are most likely to enable them to cope with these situations, there will always be a very broad margin of unpredictability. And even if the demands of a particular communication situation do not exceed those which the learners have been thoroughly prepared for, there are likely to be failures of recall, failures to activate, on the spur of the moment, certain items of knowledge or elements of skill that were acquired during the learning process.

This means that even if we were to confine ourselves to the requirements of everyday situations, predictable to a certain extent, the learner will have to be prepared to cope with unpredicted demands as well as with failures of recall.

To some people skill in coping comes naturally. Somehow they manage, whatever their lack of skill or knowledge with regard to the 'proper' forms of communication. Most people, however, will benefit substantially by being given ample opportunity, in the course of their learning process, to develop their skill in this respect. It is not primarily a matter of being 'taught' how to cope, but of being led to develop one's own strategies for doing so. Although certain strategies and techniques may almost certainly be beneficial to everyone, individual differences corresponding to differences in personality are to be given full scope.

What may be expected of learners at *Vantage* level, then, is skill in dealing with the demands of a communication situation that they are not fully prepared for. This means particularly that:

as a reader or listener the learner is not 'thrown' by the occurrence of unknown linguistic elements in a text;

as a speaker or writer the learner is prepared to seek solutions to problems caused by insufficient linguistic skill or knowledge;

as a social agent the learner is not put out by uncertainty as to the accepted code of behaviour.

There is no direct relationship between these attitudinal aspects and specific abilities. Different learners are likely to develop different sets of strategies for coping with the problems involved. Consequently, no standard operationalisation is to be sought. Yet, among the various techniques and strategies that are available a certain number may be identified as particularly likely to suit each individual learner and to contribute substantially to the development of the desired attitudes. Like other aspects of communicative ability at *Vantage* level, this may be described and listed in terms of what the learner can do, and supplemented with recommended exponents where this is appropriate. Because some items will involve the fulfilling of particular language functions and the handling of particular notions, a partial overlap with other lists in the present objective is inevitable. A similar overlap will occur between the present list and that of Chapter 9 on 'dealing with texts'.

I As a reader, the learner can:

1 deduce the meanings of complex words composed of elements (base(s) and affixes) which are familiar to the learner and which are combined in accordance with productive rules of word formation, insofar as these meanings are directly derivable on the basis of familiarity with the elements involved and with generally applied rules of word formation;

2 deduce the meanings of unfamiliar elements (particularly phrases and words) from a context of familiar elements which allows these meanings to be identified;

3 correctly interpret the meanings of so-called 'international words' that are familiar from the learner's native language and whose formal relation to the native language equivalent is fully transparent; he/she is aware of the existence of 'false friends' and will remain on the alert for differences in the meanings of international words and cognate words from one language to another;

4 find the meanings of unknown words or phrases in bilingual as well as in monolingual dictionaries;

5 with or without the aid of the above devices derive specific information from a text containing unknown elements, provided that, in addition to what is specified elsewhere in the present objective, this does not require further abilities than those listed above, the acceptable degree of difficulty of the text depending on the availability or non-availability of a dictionary.

II As a listener, the learner can:

1 carry out the operation described in I.1, provided that the word-formation process involved does not entail further phonological changes in the constituent elements than linking, stress adjustment, and consequent (regular) vowel and consonant changes;

2 carry out the operation described in I.2, provided that the contextual clues are presented in such a way that they are recognisable as such and interpretable in linear sequence without necessitating backtracking and reconsideration of the context;

3 carry out the operation described in I.3, provided that phonological differences between the foreign language form and the native language form are confined to standard correspondences between the two languages;

4 derive specific information from a text containing unknown elements, provided that, in addition to what is specified elsewhere in the present objective, this does not require further abilities than those listed in II.1, II.2 and II.3;

5 in face-to-face contacts appeal to a communication partner's assistance, particularly by using the devices listed in section 6 of Language Functions.

III　As a speaker, the learner can:

1 introduce a rephrasing
(Sorry,) I'll start again.
(Sorry,) I'll try to say that again.

2 describe by means of paraphrase, particularly by using a general word or a superordinate, with a qualification indicating

- general physical properties such as colour, size, shape (See General Notions.)

- specific features (an X with three legs)

- use (an X to cut bread)

3 describe by referring to qualities and properties

- general physical properties (See General Notions.)
  It is …

- specific features
  It has …

- use
  You can … with it.

4 identify by indicating

one like that
I'd like this, please.
I mean the one over there.

5 appeal for assistance

What do you call that (again)?
I don't know the English/German, etc. word.
In [native language] we say . . .

6 use paralinguistic means of communication (mime, gesture, facial
   expression, etc.)

IV   As a writer, the learner can:

1 express ignorance

I don't know how to say it.
I don't know what you call it.

2 use the devices mentioned under III.2 and III.3

3 use dictionaries, both bilingual and monolingual

V   As a social agent, the learner can:

1 apologise for uncertainty or ignorance as to the accepted code of
   behaviour
       I'm sorry, I don't/didn't know . . .

2 refer to what is customary in his/her own country
       In my country . . .

3 ask for guidance
       How is this done in your country?
       How should I do this?
       What should I do?
       At what time should I come?
       etc.

The above strategies and techniques are those that every learner at
Vantage level may be expected to be able to use together with the use of
the language functions listed in section 6 of Chapter 5. In addition,
each individual learner is likely to have other privileged devices at his
or her disposal. They may, but will not necessarily, include such
techniques as finding information in grammatical surveys, in general
reference works, etc., and such strategies as using a synonym for an
unknown word, allowing oneself to experiment with word formation,
foreignising a native-language form, etc. Which of these devices the
learners are given opportunities to adopt cannot be laid down in a
general objective but is to be left to those providing learning facilities
and to the learners' own initiatives.

13 Learning to learn

Vantage is an objective derived from the estimated needs of the learners as communicators. A course – that is the sum total of the learning experiences offered to the learners – designed for *Vantage* will have to enable the learners to satisfy these needs. Yet, it will inevitably do other things as well. Depending on its design and presentation it may give the learners pleasure or hardship, it may promote, maintain, or reduce their motivation for learning, it may bolster or diminish their self-confidence, it may stimulate their interest and sensitivity to the world around them or it may cause them to withdraw into themselves. In short, it may benefit the learners far beyond the basic objectives of the course or it may limit itself to these and, possibly, it may even harm the learners as individuals. All these effects – positive or negative – are independent of the learning load that is represented by the content of an objective; they are produced by the impact upon particular learners of the forms and the manners of the presentation and the practice of this content. At the same time they may affect the learners' impression of the learning load in making this load appear to be more demanding or less so.

The experience, then, of learning for *Vantage* will affect the learners in various ways beyond the acquisition of a certain learning content. One of the ways in which it may substantially benefit the learners is in stimulating their awareness of the learning process itself and increasing their learning potential. This 'learning to learn' does not, at first sight, appear to fall within our communicative objective. It may, however, easily be integrated into this objective. And there are at least two good reasons for trying to do so. In the first place, it has now long been accepted by learning psychologists that insightful learning is likely to be more effective – and to produce more lasting effects – than learning without insight. This greater effectiveness is partly due to the motivating power of knowing what one is doing and why one is doing it. Secondly, 'learning to learn' is an invaluable aspect of preparing the learners for whatever further learning may be required by them. Like any general objective, *Vantage* is no more than an assessment of what the average member of a particular target group is most likely to need at a given stage in his or her development. The actual needs of individual members of the target group are certain to differ to a greater or a lesser extent from those of the fictitious 'average member'. This means that in order to be adequately equipped for independent functioning in and with the foreign language, learners should have the insights and know-how required for bridging the gap between their individual needs and those provided for in the specifications of the general objective. And even if the gap is so wide that the learners may have to seek professional guidance, some insight into their own learning potential and in how to exploit this most effectively will be of considerable advantage to them.

Finally it should be said that the promotion of learner autonomy is a fundamental objective of the communicative approach adopted by the Council of Europe. That is to say the learners should be encouraged and enabled to take increasing charge of their own learning and to develop the attitudes, knowledge, understanding and skills which will enable them to do so. Insofar as *Vantage* is a statement of a learning objective and not just a description of a certain level of proficiency, the skills involved in learning to learn are not simply a by-product of some courses, but an essential aspect of that objective, which all teaching towards that objective should promote. As such they form an integral part of the objective, not an optional extra.

Thus, in describing what learners should be able to do with and through the use of language for communication, we legitimately take into account their use of the experience of language learning to become more efficient and effective language learners as well as language users. It is part of the *Vantage* objective for learners to be willing and able to engage in the struggle to communicate in the situations confronting them with the resources and strategies they command, taking the risk of error, inviting and welcoming various forms of assistance from more experienced interlocutors and, systematically, to learn from the experience. It is also part of the objective that learners should actively seek opportunities for engaging in such encounters, exploiting not only the presence of native speakers in the environment but also the opportunities offered by radio and television broadcasts as well as printed and recorded material.

'Learning to learn', as we said above, should be incorporated into the *Vantage* objective, not as an additional objective that will affect the pragmatic/linguistic content but as one that is to be achieved through the form and manner of presentation and practice of this content or, indeed, through the individual's experience of the language. We shall formulate the learning-to-learn component in terms of a learning objective, but at a fairly high level of generality, leaving scope for a range of concrete realisations by individual learners with possibly different learning styles.

The learning-to-learn objective

I **Concerning needs and objectives**

1 The learners are aware of the nature of their communicative needs.

2 The learners are aware of the nature of the learning objective offered to them.

3 The learners have insight into the degree of relevance to their communicative needs of the learning objective offered to them.

4 In the areas covered by Chapter 7 (Topic-related tasks and lexicon) the learners are able to identify, learn and use the terms specific to their own needs and interests.

5 The learners can identify those of their communication needs, if any, which are not catered for in the objective offered to them.

6 The learners can describe, in general terms, additional objectives which will satisfy the needs referred to under 5 above and/or they can recognise the relevance to these needs of further objectives offered to them.
I'd like to read articles about economics.
I'd like to write business letters.

II   Concerning learning processes

1 The learners are familiar with the possibility of dividing an overall learning task into a number of sub-tasks, each with its own objective.

2 The learners are familiar with the distinctions between productive ability and receptive ability and with the difference in degree of skill that may be required in order to meet the needs for each type of ability.

3 The learners are aware of the contributions of pragmatic, grammatical, lexical and phonological adequacy to communicative effectiveness.

4 The learners can identify the roles (acquisition of knowledge, of insight, of skill) of various types of learning materials and are aware of the potential relevance of such materials to the achievement of their objective.

5 The learners know how to find information about usage (e.g. in dictionaries, relevant reference works and reference grammars).

6 The learners have experienced various methods of vocabulary acquisition and have identified one or more that they consider particularly useful to themselves.

7 The learners are aware of the potential of learning through exposure to foreign language use and know how various compensation strategies may enable them to cope with texts containing unknown elements.

III Concerning learning from direct experience of the language

1 The learners are able to engage in communicative interaction using the resources and strategies specified at *Vantage* level and to learn from experience.

2 The learners are able to observe the language and strategies used by a more experienced interlocutor and thus increase their own repertory of responses, receptive and productive.

3 The learners are, for instance, able as listeners and as readers to perceive, memorise and note down words and expressions not previously encountered, noting also their situational context and functional/notional value.

4 The learners are able to repeat back new words and expressions which occur in conversations in which they participate, to make use of them themselves as soon as appropriate and, by later making notes if necessary, add them to their repertory.

5 The learners are able to experiment with forms of expression (e.g. by recombining known words and grammatical structures, or rules of word and structure formation), to note their acceptance or non-acceptance by more experienced speakers and, if need be, to modify the rules they operate.

6 The learners are able to employ compensation and repair strategies (cf. section 6 of Chapter 5), noting, learning and using new language supplied by their interlocutor.

IV Concerning evaluation

1 The learners can monitor their progress towards the terminal objective, particularly by relating their communicative ability to successive intermediate objectives.

2 The learners are aware of the role of formative assessment as an aid to the planning of further learning activities.

The above analysis of 'learning to learn' is based on assumptions as to what may reasonably be expected to be feasible for foreign language learners without diverting too much of their attention from the actual task of learning to use the language itself.

Several of the above items are formulated as 'the learners are aware of...'. This obviously allows for different degrees of awareness, and no attempt is made to operationalise this concept. This simply means that, in our view, courses meant to lead up to *Vantage* level should provide learners with the opportunity to develop the awareness concerned without, however, making specific demands upon the learners in this respect.

Note The present chapter duplicates, to a large extent, the corresponding chapters in *Waystage 1990* and *Threshold 1990*. Learners who have proceeded through these two earlier objectives are likely to have already acquired the skills and attitudes mentioned here before continuing to *Vantage*. Others, however, who have acquired their previous foreign language ability in a different way, may still benefit considerably by what is described in this chapter, and, indeed, will need the skills and attitudes concerned in order to achieve full *Vantage* ability.

14 Degree of skill

Since, as we have remarked repeatedly in previous chapters, *Vantage*, as compared to *Threshold*, is marked by a relaxation of constraints, learners at *Vantage* level may be expected to communicate not only more effectively but also more efficiently and with greater ease in most of the communication situations in which they may find themselves. From one learner to another these situations, and their demands, may vary considerably, and they are even largely unpredictable. This means that at *Vantage* level learners should have a degree of communicative skill that enables them to cope with the unforeseen, and not just to cope but to do this without being unduly hindered by gaps in their ability to use the foreign language. This requirement may be defined under the headings of *accuracy*, *appropriacy* and *fluency*. These concepts are composite ones which can only be used with some measure of reliability in judging candidates if they are further specified and if a balanced weighting of their components is ensured.

Accuracy involves:

- pronunciation (including rhythm and intonation);

- spelling;

- lexical, idiomatic and grammatical correctness.

At *Vantage* level learners may be expected – and will expect themselves – to score high on each of these points. Thus, their pronunciation will in no way interfere with being easily understood by native speakers of the foreign language as well as by non-native speakers with a communicative ability corresponding to or above that described in *Threshold 1990*. This does not mean that they should not have a detectable foreign accent so that more experienced native speakers may well be able to make a good guess as to the nature of their L1. At this level, however, it does mean that also native speakers with little or no experience of communication with foreigners should have no difficulty in understanding them. Occasional repeats may have to be asked for, though never to such an extent that communication becomes laborious.

When *Vantage* learners express themselves in writing, a closer approximation to the foreign language norm may be expected than in speech. Spelling mistakes will be either absent or rare. Not only will the learners have acquired sound spelling habits, but in cases where there is doubt they will, given time, usually be able to solve their problem by consulting a dictionary or otherwise by choosing an alternative structure. This relatively high level of correctness is desirable if the learners – as writers – wish to be taken seriously as reasonably well-educated people.

At *Vantage* level more importance may properly be attached to formal correctness in the use of lexicon, idiom and grammar than was the case at *Threshold* level. By now the learners will be familiar with at least the more commonly used grammatical structures and skilled in using them for their own purposes. They will rarely produce ungrammatical forms and their comprehension in this area will be complete, except, of course, if such highly formal language is used that native speakers, too, may have comprehension problems or, in the case of spoken language, if irregularities in the signal (e.g. false starts, distorted structures) lead to diminished intelligibility.

As regards lexicon and idiom the situation is less ambiguous. In the case of pronunciation, as we noted, full intelligibility in spite of a detectable foreign accent may, for many learners, be acceptable, even as a terminal level. When it comes to lexicon and idiom, however, learners may easily feel hampered if there are noticeable gaps in their ability. In principle, they should be able to deal adequately with everyday requirements as well as with those matters that are of particular interest to them. However, doing this not only effectively but also correctly and with the desired ease may occasionally demand more lexical and idiomatic skill than can be expected even at *Vantage* level. An adequate use of repair strategies should have become second nature by now, but this will not always help the learners to avoid communication problems entirely. What may be expected at this level is the ability to cope adequately and with a high degree of correctness with the demands of those communication situations that the learners may reasonably expect to find themselves in, and a sufficient command of a variety of strategies to avail themselves of in cases where their command of lexicon and/or idiom falls short of the requirements of the situation. By now the learners should have enough insight into the process of the acquisition of lexicon and idiom to be prompted by such experiences to continue their efforts to increase their possibilities in these areas. On the whole, at *Vantage* level learners may be expected to achieve such a degree of correctness that they are able to satisfy their communication needs without feeling hindered by a sense of inadequacy. They should realise, however, that occasionally they are likely to express themselves in a somewhat awkward manner – particularly when it comes to the use of idiomatic expressions and to the choice of appropriate lexical synonyms – and, equally, that occasional misunderstanding of a communication partner's intention cannot be entirely ruled out.

Appropriacy involves:

- sociolinguistic appropriacy;
- sociocultural appropriacy;

- social appropriacy.

At *Vantage* level the learners should have a high degree of awareness of the importance of these three types of appropriacy with a view to the achievement of successful communication. They will be sufficiently skilled with regard to the first two types to ensure adequate participation in communication events, including those where native speakers are involved, and with regard to the third they will have strategies at their disposal enabling them to contribute to a successful outcome of encounters with native speakers as well as non-native speakers of the foreign language. Sociolinguistic appropriacy involves such matters as role adequacy, register and the realisation of 'intentions', and sociocultural appropriacy refers to the adequacy of use of the sociocultural reference frame. These two types may be acquired by all learners through application, study and practice. The achievement of social appropriacy, i.e. the adequacy of the handling of interpersonal contacts, is only partly a matter of deliberate application and depends to a considerable extent on personality features which are not directly under the learners' control. It is, therefore, less suitable as a criterion to be fairly used in evaluating the learners' progress in foreign language acquisition.

Fluency, which term may be used for productive as well as receptive ability, involves:

- ease of access to and retrieval from memory;
- command of discourse strategies;
- rate of delivery and processing.

Although individual learners will vary considerably in the degree of fluency that may be achieved by them – as is the case in their native language – their fluency at *Vantage* will be such that unnaturally long pauses in production and extreme delays in interpretation will be rare. This means not only that their command of the linguistic apparatus (grammar, vocabulary, etc.) is adequate for most purposes but also that their compensatory competence (i.e. adequacy in using repair strategies and avoidance strategies) is sufficiently developed to enable them to continue the flow of communicative interaction in spite of gaps in their linguistic ability.

To sum up, at *Vantage* level the learners will have achieved a degree of skill that gives them the confidence that they can cope adequately with the requirements of the large majority of those communicative situations, foreseen or unforeseen, that they are likely to find themselves in. 'Coping adequately' requires that degree of foreign language ability that enables them to achieve a successful outcome without being unduly hindered by the need to use the foreign language.

15 By-products

In a different context (Learning to learn, see Chapter 13) we noted that, in addition to enabling the learners to satisfy their estimated needs, a course designed for *Vantage* will 'inevitably do other things as well'. Some of these things may (have to) be deliberately planned for in the course. 'Learning to learn' is one of these; the acquisition of adequate compensation strategies (see Chapter 12) is another. Other things, however, will automatically follow from the experience of learning for *Vantage* without any provisions having been made for them in the course offered to the learners and even without their having been explicitly included in the objective concerned. They are simply what we may regard as 'by-products' of a successful learning experience. This does not mean to say that they could not figure more centrally, or even be the main concern, of other objectives for foreign language learning with a different orientation from that of the *Waystage–Threshold–Vantage* series. In the present chapter, by way of exemplification, we shall briefly discuss two of such by-products: literary appreciation and mediation skill.

By 'literary appreciation' we mean here 'the ability to understand literary products and to experience – possibly even to evaluate – their impacts'. In the objective for *Vantage*, notably in Chapter 9 (Dealing with texts), nothing is said about literary texts. Nor, however, are they explicitly excluded. In fact, all of the criteria 'for the delimitation of the range of texts that learners may be expected to be able to deal with' which are listed in Chapter 9 are satisfied by numerous literary texts. Thus it may be expected that at *Vantage* level the learners' command of English is such as to enable them to read, and enjoy, many short stories, novels, poems, etc. Since this will be the case even if they have not been specifically prepared for the reading of literary works there is no need to mention this ability explicitly in the present objective. This does not mean that a course including the experience of dealing with works of literature could not provide richer and more rewarding stimuli to the learners than one without it. Nor does it deny the possibility of increased learning effects due to the memorisation of (fragments of) literary texts, particularly verse texts. However, such learning experiences are not specifically demanded by our objective.

Another by-product of learning for *Vantage* is a certain degree of mediation skill. 'Mediation' is the term used in the Council of Europe's *Common European Framework of Reference for Languages: learning, teaching, assessment* (Cambridge: Cambridge University Press, in press) for those language activities where 'the language user is not concerned to express his/her own meanings, but simply to act as an intermediary between interlocutors who are unable to understand each other directly, normally (but not exclusively) speakers of different languages'. Mediation may involve such activities as simultaneous interpretation, consecutive interpretation, exact translation (contracts, legal and scientific texts, etc.), literary translation, summarising gist (within L2 or between L1 and L2), paraphrasing, etc. While it will be clear that the ability to carry out most of these activities can only be acquired through long and intensive study and practice in specially designed courses, for which separate objectives may be formulated, a certain degree of mediation skill will develop as a by-product of learning for *Vantage* level. This will especially be the case with the type of mediation indicated in the *Framework* as 'informal interpretation'. This may involve, according to the same source, interpretation

- for friends, family, clients, foreign guests, etc.

- of foreign visitors in own country

- of native speakers when abroad

- in social and transactional situations

- of signs, menus, notices, etc.

Such language activities will often take the form of a response to

- What did he/she say?

- What does it say here/there?

- Tell him/her that ...

- Ask him/her if ...

It may be assumed that the foreign language ability of learners at *Vantage* level will be such that responses of this kind are well within their capability, as well as summarising the gist of, for instance, newspaper and magazine articles accessible to themselves for the benefit of someone unfamiliar with the foreign language concerned. The acquisition of this kind of mediation skill does not depend on special learning and/or teaching efforts beyond those which are needed to acquire *Vantage* ability as described elsewhere in this document. In other words, it need not be separately included in the formulation of the objective itself, nor will it have to play a role in any evaluation procedures that may be related to it. Thus, it is simply a by-product of learning for *Vantage* level.

Appendix A Lexical exponents of specific notions for *Vantage*

This appendix is a listing of lexical exponents of specific notions which those concerned with the raising of communicative ability up to *Vantage* with regard to the 'themes' of *Threshold* might wish to consider. The exponents listed here are not presented as a defined lexical syllabus, nor even as 'recommended exponents'. They represent stimuli which may be found useful by those involved in the development of theme-related ability to *Vantage*. Together with the common-core elements listed in Chapters 5 and 6 under 'language functions' and 'general notions', the lexicon contained in this appendix should provide learners with a significantly more advanced linguistic apparatus for dealing with the themes of most likely general interest to them than was available at *Threshold* level.

In accordance with its intended role the list presented here is to a large extent open-ended. The majority of the lexical items contained in it are listed as members of open classes, to be reduced, expanded, or otherwise altered as may best suit the needs and interests of the learners. To remind the user of this, they are invariably preceded by **e.g.** following the general indication of the class. Thus, those wishing some guidance as to which 'names of birds' (2.8) to consider for inclusion in a *Vantage* programme will find those which the authors of the present specification think may be particularly useful to them without, however, wishing to impose any selection on them. If anybody may wonder why, for instance, the penguin and the puffin have been included and not the pelican, they are, of course, entirely free to follow their own inclination. In fact, the present list is simply meant to stimulate them to do this.

The list includes all the exponents 'recommended' for *Threshold*. Whether or not users are familiar with this earlier objective, they should have no difficulty in finding their way in it. The exponents are presented under the same headings and sub-headings as was the case in *Threshold* with exponents of one and the same specific notion listed thus: **first name/Christian name/forename/given name**, and exponents of related but different notions thus: **fax, fax number**. Names of open classes are indicated: *names of plants, trees, flowers*; those of closed sets thus: names of letters of the alphabet

1 Personal identification

1.1 name
name
first name/Christian
name/forename/given
name
surname/family name
initials
titles e.g. Mr . . ., Mrs . . .,
Miss . . ., Ms . . ., Lord . . .,
Lady . . ., Sir . . ., Dame . . .,
Reverend . . ., Captain . . .,
Major . . ., Colonel . . ., Dr . . .,
Professor . . ., . . . B.A.,
. . . M.A., . . . B.Sc., . . . Ph.D.
to write/to spell (as in: How
do you write/spell your
name?)
names of letters of the
alphabet
to call (as in: We call him Bill.)
to be/to be called (as in: He is
(called) Bill.)
to sign
signature
letter (as in: What is the last
letter of your name?)
nickname

1.2 address
to live (as in: Where do you
live?)
address (as in: What is your
address?)
names of roads, etc. e.g.
park, road, square, street,
alley, avenue, circus, lane,
terrace
number (as in: I live at
number fifteen.)
cardinal numerals (as
required)
postal code
e-mail address
village
town/city

country
names of countries (as
required)
names of cities (as required)

1.3 telephone number
(See also 11.2.)
telephone
**to call/to phone, to ring
up/to make a (phone)call/to
give (a person) a call**
telephone number
0 (pronounced [əʊ] in
telephone numbers)
fax, fax number
to fax

1.4 date and place of birth
to be born (as in: I was born
in London on . . .)
date
place (of birth)
birthday
names of the months
numerals (as required)

1.5 age
See General Notions 5.1.10.

1.6 sex
sex
man, woman
boy, girl
male, female
m., f. (reading only)
gentlemen/gents, ladies (as
on lavatory doors)

1.7 marital status
(not/un-)married, single
bachelor, spinster
divorced
separated
engaged (to be married)
fiancé(e)
widow, widower
partner
marriage
wedding anniversary

1.8   **nationality**
national, nationality
names of nationalities
citizen (as in: He is a British
citizen.), citizenship
foreign, foreigner
(non)-resident
native (as in: He is a native of
Wales.)
asylum seeker, refugee
emigrant, to emigrate,
emigration
immigrant, to immigrate,
immigration
migrant
colony, colonial

1.9   **origin**
to be from .../ to come
from ...

1.10   **occupation**
job/occupation/profession
to do (as in: What do you do
(for a living)?)
to be (as in: He is a
technician.)
names of occupations e.g.
baker, builder, businessman,
businesswoman, butcher,
carpenter, civil servant,
clergyman, clerk, doctor/
physician, engineer, farm
worker, greengrocer, grocer,
housewife, labourer,
mechanic, miner, nurse, office
worker, pilot, (computer-)
programmer, sailor, salesman,
saleswoman, scientist,
secretary, shop assistant,
shopkeeper, social worker,
soldier, teacher, technician,
therapist, tradesman, typist
names of places of work
e.g. factory, farm, hospital,
laboratory, office, school, shop
*names of occupational
activities* e.g. to build, to buy,

to teach, to sell, to work (as
in: I work in an office.)
to be in business
learned professions
craft(s)
trade
staff (as in: She is a member
of the staff.)
board (as in: She is on the
board.)
director
boss/chief/employer/
manager
white-collar job,
white-collar worker
worker/employee
au pair
temp, temp office
firm/company
employment bureau/
employment agency
volunteer, voluntary work
to produce, production
goods

1.11   **family**
family (as in: Have you
brought your family?; Have
you any family?)
parents/father and mother
child
baby
husband, wife
orphan
an only child
stepchild, stepfather,
stepmother
to adopt, adoption
names of relatives e.g. aunt,
brother, cousin, daughter,
father, grandchild,
grandfather, grandmother,
great grandfather, etc.,
...-in-law, in-laws, mother,
nephew, niece, sister, son,
uncle

1.12 religion
religion
names of religions e.g.
Buddhism, Christianity,
Judaism, Hinduism, Islam
names of followers of
various religions e.g.
Buddhist, Christian, Jew,
Hindu, Muslim, Protestant,
Roman Catholic
names of places of worship
e.g. abbey, chapel, church,
cathedral, mosque,
synagogue, temple
to believe (in ...)
clergy
names of members of the
clergy **e.g.** archbishop,
bishop, minister, pope, priest,
rabbi, rector, vicar
god, God
service (as in: There are three
services on Sundays.)

1.13 likes and dislikes
See Language Functions
2.5.16–2.5.18; objects of
likes and dislikes to be
derived from other themes.

1.14 character, disposition,
temperament
What sort of ...? (as in: What
sort of man/woman/child, etc.
is he/she?)
character
traits of character,
disposition, temperament
e.g. active, aggressive,
arrogant, bad, bad-tempered,
bore **(as in:** He is a terrible
bore.), boring, clever, cynic,
cynical, depressive, dull,
emotional, energetic,
enterprising, enthusiastic, evil,
fool, foolish, friendly, good,
generous, impulsive,
intelligent, kind, lazy,

naughty, nice, obedient,
optimist, optimistic, pessimist,
pessimistic, pleasant, quiet,
restless, sarcastic, selfish, shy,
silly, spoilt, stubborn, stupid,
superficial, timid,
unintelligent, unkind,
unpleasant, unselfish
sexual inclination **e.g.**
bisexual, heterosexual, gay,
homosexual, lesbian

1.15 physical appearance
indications of physical
appearance **e.g.** beautiful,
fat, handsome, lovely, plain,
pretty, sexy, short, slim, tall,
thin, ugly; bald, dark-haired,
fair-haired, red-haired

2 House and home,
environment

2.1 types of accommodation
accommodation
names of places to live in
e.g. house, country house,
town house, council house,
terrace house, semi-detached,
detached, bungalow, cottage,
residence, farmhouse,
apartment, flat, block of flats,
towerblock, skyscraper,
building, boarding-house,
bed-sitter, (un)furnished
room(s)
to buy, to rent

2.2 accommodation, rooms
room (as in: We have two
rooms on the ground floor.
We have plenty of room here.)
names of rooms **e.g.**
bathroom, bedroom, cellar,
drawing room, guest room,
library, hall, kitchen,
lavatory/toilet/w.c., living

room, sitting room, study,
utility room
names of parts of a house
e.g. basement, floor **(as in:**
The bedrooms are on the first
floor. We have a marble floor
in our bathroom.**)**, ground
floor, top floor, attic, roof,
shed, garage; ceiling,
window, door, wall,
cupboard, lift, balcony,
terrace
garden
downstairs (as in: The
kitchen is downstairs. Let's go
downstairs.**), upstairs (as in:**
The bathroom is upstairs. Let's
go upstairs.**)**

2.3   **furniture, bedclothes,
decoration**
furniture
*names of pieces of
furniture* **e.g.** bed, chair,
desk, lamp, table, bookcase,
wardrobe, dressing-table
names of bedclothes **e.g.**
blanket, sheet, quilt,
bedspread, eiderdown,
pillow, pillowcase
mattress
sleeping bag
carpet
curtain
wallpaper
mirror
picture
painting
plant
poster

2.4   **cost**
(See also General Notions
5.2.1.)
price
to be (as in: The room is £55
per week.**)**
rent, to rent

to let (as in: Rooms to let.**),
for sale (as in:** House for
sale.**)
included (as in:** Water is
included in the rent.**)
mortgage
deposit**

2.5   **services**
**electricity, plug, socket,
adaptor, wire, fuse
gas
heating, central heating
telephone
water
on (as in:** The heating is on.**),
off (as in:** The heating is off.**)
to turn/switch on/off
switch (as in:** Where is the
switch?**)**

2.6   **amenities**
**bath, shower
washing machine,
dishwasher
sink
tap
refrigerator/fridge, freezer
(gas) cooker
radio, television, CD player,
video recorder
vacuum cleaner
stove, open fire, fireplace,
gas fire, electric heater
to clean (as in:** The rooms are
cleaned twice a week.**)
to wash (as in:** You can wash
your clothes downstairs.**)**

2.7   **region and geographical
features**
area, part of the country
names of types of areas **e.g.**
urban, rural, countryside,
farmlands, fields, industrial,
meadows, mining,
forest/wood, jungle, hill, hilly,
moor, mountain,

mountainous, sea, ocean, seaside, coast, shore, beach, peninsula, island, lake, valley
names of regional features **e.g.** farm, dairy farm, cattle, cattle-breeding, greenhouse, horticulture, agriculture, industry, mine, factory, canal, river, bay, dune, cliff, dike
soil
names of types of soil e.g. clay, mud, peat, pebble, sand
names of geographical notions e.g. earth, globe, global, continent, continental, equator, hemisphere, tropics, tropical, subtropics, subtropical
top (as in: We could see the tops of the mountains.)
bottom (as in: We could see the bottom of the lake.)
flat (as in: Our part of the country is quite flat.)

2.8   flora and fauna
animal, bird, fish, insect, pet
names of animals, birds, fishes, insects e.g. badger, bear, cat, cow, dog, elephant, fox, goat, hare, horse, lion, monkey, pig, rabbit, sheep, squirrel, tiger, wolf; duck, eagle, goose, (sea-)gull, owl, parrot, peacock, penguin, pheasant, pigeon, puffin, robin, sparrow, starling, swallow, swan; cod, eel, haddock, herring, plaice, salmon, sole, trout; ant, bee, butterfly, flea, fly, louse, mosquito, moth, wasp
plant, tree, flower, shrub
names of plants, trees, flowers e.g. corn, grass, heather, wheat; beech, birch, chestnut, fir, oak, pine,

willow, yew; anemone, bluebell, buttercup, daffodil, daisy, dahlia, dandelion, hyacinth, iris, lily, pansy, rose, snowdrop, tulip

....

3   Daily life

3.1   at home
(See also section 4.)
sleep, to sleep
dream, to dream, nightmare
awake, to wake up
to get up
to be busy, to work hard
to wash, to take a bath, to take a shower
to brush one's teeth
to comb one's hair
to shave
to get (un)dressed
to have breakfast, etc.
meal
names of meals e.g. breakfast, lunch, tea, dinner, supper
chores
to cook (as in: I shall cook dinner for you.)
to prepare breakfast, etc.
to make tea, coffee, etc.
to lay the table
to wash up/to do the washing up
to tidy up, to dust, to vacuum clean
to make the beds
to do the laundry, to iron
to water (as in: Shall I water the plants?)
to clean (as in: I clean the windows once a week.)
to go shopping, to do the shopping

to go to school, to go to
work, to go home
to come home
to take (the dog) for a walk
to go to bed, to go to sleep
spare time

3.2 at work
(See also 1.10.)
working hours
to start (stop) work
(to work) full time, part time
permanent
(temporary) employment
break
holidays, days off (as in: We
have two days off a week.)
(on) leave
to be free (as in: We are free
on Saturdays.)
free (as in: We get a free meal
every day.)
canteen
colleague
strike/industrial action, go
slow
unemployment,
unemployed
unemployment benefit
on the dole
to be fired/dismissed/made
redundant
to retire, retirement
trade union
social security, social
benefits

3.3 income
income/salary/wages
pocket money
grant, allowance
(old age) pension
tax(es), rates
to earn

3.4 schooling
See Specific Notions,
section 8.

3.5 prospects
to become (as in: I may
become a doctor.)
to learn, to study
to qualify as
to apply for (as in: I won't
apply for that job.)
career

···

**4 Free time,
entertainments and
pursuits**

4.1 leisure
to be free (as in: I'm free after
six.)
free time/spare time/
leisure
holiday(s)
bank holiday
to go out

4.2 hobbies and interests
(See also Language
Functions 2.4 and
2.5.16–2.5.18.)
hobby, interests
to be interested in ...
names of hobbies e.g.
carpentry, collecting stamps,
fishing, gardening, knitting,
photography, sailing
names of fields of interest
e.g. computers, films, music,
politics, sports
to go for ... (as in: I always go
for a walk, swim, **etc.** on
Sundays.)

4.3 radio, TV, etc.
radio/wireless
to listen to (the radio)
television/TV, cable
television, satellite
television
to watch (TV)
listener, viewer

network
channel
programme
*names of radio/TV
programmes* e.g. comedy,
commercials, current affairs,
documentary, drama, film,
interview, news, quiz, soap
(to) broadcast
to show (as in: What are they
showing on TV tonight?)
live (broadcast,
programme)
**announcer, reporter,
interviewer, quiz master**
**cassette recorder,
tape-recorder**
cassette, tape
tape deck
Walkman
video recorder, videotape
record/gramophone
record, record player
CD/compact disc, CD player
loudspeaker/speaker
microphone/mike
earphones/headphones
tuner
to play (as in: Let's play your
new record.)
song, music
names of types of music
e.g. classical, folk, house
music, jazz, modern music,
pop music
volume, sound
to turn up/down (the
volume)
loud, soft
bass, treble

4.4   **cinema, theatre, concert,
etc.**
*names of places of public
entertainment* e.g. cabaret,
cinema, circus, disco,
night-club, theatre

*names of public
performances* e.g. ballet,
concert, film, floorshow,
musical, opera, revue, show
*names of types of
performers* e.g. acrobat,
actor, actress, ballet dancer,
clown, disc jockey, (film) star,
musician, pop star, singer
*names of musical
instruments* e.g. bagpipe,
clarinet, drum, flute, guitar,
harp, horn, organ, piano,
saxophone, trombone,
trumpet, violin
to dance
to play (as in: Who is playing
Hamlet? She plays the guitar.)
to sing
performance
festival
(to) queue
ticket (as in: I'll get the
tickets.)
ticket office, booking office
**afternoon performance,
matinée**
rehearsal, dress rehearsal
seat
names of types of seats e.g.
stalls, box, balcony, upper
circle, dress circle
row (as in: We have seats in
row five.)
front, centre, back (as in: We
have seats in the front, centre,
at the back.)
stage
foyer
**entrance, exist, emergency
exit**
cloakroom
lavatory/toilet/w.c.
programme (as in: Shall I buy
a programme?)
interval
drama, comedy, tragedy

act, scene (as in: Act 4,
scene 1)
conductor
choir
producer
script
circus
orchestra

4.5   exhibitions, museums, etc.
museum, gallery, art gallery
art, artist, work of art
exhibition
picture/painting, drawing,
etching, oil painting,
watercolour
portrait
sculpture, statue
pottery
tapestry
modern, old, antique
showcase
open-air museum
visitor
guide, guided tour
guard
opening-hours, open (as in:
Open on Sundays 2–5 pm.)
closing time, to close

4.6   photography
photograph, photographer,
photography
to take pictures/photos
slide
film
camera, video camera
screen
lens
battery
to expose, exposure
to develop, to print (a film)
to enlarge, enlargement

**4.7   intellectual and artistic
         pursuits**
to read
to study, to learn

book
story, short story
poem
names of types of books
e.g. biography, detective
story, novel, short story, spy
story, thriller
bookshop
library
to write, author/writer
poet, poetry
prose
playwright/dramatist
literature
publisher, publication
editor, edition
volume
title
cover
preface
chapter
page
paperback, hard cover
plot
character, main/principal
character
subject
copy (as in: There are only a
few copies left.)
out of print
names of art forms e.g.
painting, photography,
sculpture
*names of practitioners of
various art forms* e.g.
architect, painter,
photographer, sculptor

4.8   sports
sport(s)
names of sports and games
e.g. baseball, chess, cricket,
football, hockey, (horse)
racing, riding, rugby, skiing,
snooker, swimming, (lawn)
tennis

names of practitioners of various sports e.g. athlete, boxer, cyclist, football player
to play (as in: I've never played hockey.)
(playing-)cards
race, to race
game, match (as in: The next match is between England and France.), **home match, away match**
to train, training, trainer
goal, goalkeeper
to score
half-time
draw (as in: The game ended in a draw.)
result
player
coach, manager (as in: He used to be the coach/manager of Real Madrid.)
team
club
referee
champion
league
bookmaker
field, ground
stadium
(golf) course
indoor, outdoor
skating rink
swimming pool
tennis court
ball
against (as in: We saw England against France in '68.)

4.9 **press**
to publish, publication
names of types of periodical publications e.g. newspaper, paper, daily/daily paper, weekly, monthly, magazine, quality paper, tabloid

pamphlet, brochure
issue
article
picture, illustration
advertisement
review, report
item
headline(s)
letter to the editor
editorial
crossword
page, front page, back page
names of types of press contributors e.g. editor, reporter, journalist, free-lance journalist, correspondent, critic, columnist, cartoonist, illustrator
to read
to print
to report
to subscribe, subscriber, subscription
circulation

....

5 Travel

5.1 **public transport**
to go (as in: How can I go to Liverpool?), **to travel, traveller, to travel by air, train, bus, etc., to fly, to make a cruise**
passenger
trip, journey, voyage
to catch (train, flight, etc.)
names of means of public transport e.g. aeroplane/plane, helicopter, bus, coach, train, underground, fast train, slow train, tram, boat, ferry, ship, taxi/cab
names of boarding places e.g. airport, terminal, gate,

bus stop, tram stop, (railway) station, platform, quay, harbour, taxi rank/cab rank
names of members of transport staff e.g. crew, pilot, captain, steward, stewardess/(air)hostess, driver, guard, taxi driver/cab driver
names of types of ticket e.g. ticket, season ticket, single **(as in:** Two singles to Brighton, please.**), return ticket, adult;** first, second, **etc.** class, business class, tourist class, economy class
airline
to check in
to board, boarding-pass
to fly, flight (as in: Your flight is from terminal A. Enjoy your flight.**), charter flight**
security (as in: security check**)**
railways
carriage, compartment, seat, cabin
to change (as in: For Leeds you have to change at Sheffield.**)**
direction (as in: Leeds is in the opposite direction.**)**
connection (as in: We shall miss our connection to Reading.**)**
tunnel
booking-office, to book
timetable
fare (as in: What's the fare to Liverpool?**), reduced fare**
to smoke, non-smoking
waiting-room, lounge
arrival, departure
luggage/baggage
lost property office
travel bureau/travel agency
information, information

office, information desk, enquiries
restaurant, bar, refreshments
delay, to be delayed
cancellation, to cancel

5.2   **private transport**
(See also 5.3 and 11.8–11.9.)
names of vehicles e.g. bike/bicycle, car, lorry, motor cycle, scooter, van
to drive, driver
to ride
cyclist, motorist
to hire/to rent (as in: We could always rent a car.**)**

5.3   **traffic**
(See also 5.3.)
traffic
names of types of roads e.g. street, one-way street, road, main road, motorway, bridge, flyover, roundabout
to park, carpark, blue zone
subway
to cross, crossing, level crossing
corner
traffic lights
speed, speed limit
fine (as in: You'll have to pay a fine of £30.**)**
driving licence
danger, dangerous
safe, safety, safety belt
signpost
to follow (as in: Follow the signs.**)**
pedestrian, pedestrian precinct/zone
pavement
map, road map
distance
to lose one's way
route

common road-sign texts
e.g. cross now, exit, get in
lane, give way, keep left/right,
no parking, no waiting, no
U-turn, one way, turn
left/right, dual carriageway
ahead

5.4   holidays
tour, tourism, tourist
excursion, guided tour
tourist office, tourist guide
group (as in: We went with a
group of tourists.)
to visit
sights, sightseeing
names of sights and
buildings of interest e.g.
abbey, castle, cathedral,
church, museum, park, ruins,
stately home, palace, zoo
abroad/to a foreign country
(as in: Are you going abroad/
to a foreign country this year?)
names of continents:
Africa, America, Antarctica,
Asia, Australia, Europe

5.5   accommodation
accommodation
to stay at/with
names of types of
accommodation for
travellers e.g. camp site,
caravan, guest house, inn,
hotel, motel, tent, youth
hostel
names of features of hotel
rooms e.g. single room,
double room, family room,
balcony, view, minibar,
private facilities, en suite
full board, half board, bed
and breakfast
full breakfast, continental
breakfast
to book, reservation
deposit

names of parts of a hotel
e.g. reception, hall, lounge,
lift, swimming pool,
emergency exit, fire escape
receptionist, to register,
registration form (hall)
porter
desk (as in: Please leave your
key at the desk.)
key
to call (as in: Can you call me
at six, please?)
to disturb (as in: Do not
disturb.)
room service
message (as in: Is there a
message for me?)
to press, button (as in: Press
the button for the third floor.)
to push, to pull (as in:
Push/pull to open the door.)
to check in/out
bill
charge, price
included, inclusive
receipt
to pay cash, by cheque, with
a credit card
account (as in: The price of
the meal will be put on your
account.)
dormitory
cot
sleeping bag
regulations

5.6   luggage
luggage/baggage
names of pieces of luggage
e.g. bag, travelling bag, box,
handbag, suitcase, rucksack.
to pack
locker

5.7   entering and leaving a
country
frontier/border
immigration

passport control, visa
customs, customs office
to import, to export
to declare (as in: Have you
anything to declare?)
to open (as in: Will you open
your bag, please?)
duty (as in: You'll have to pay
duty on this.)
duty free
money
to change (as in: I want to
change $500.)
rate of exchange, currency

5.8   travel documents
document
passport, visa
valid
insurance
driving licence

....

**6   Relations with other
         people**

6.1   relationship
relationship
names of relationships e.g.
acquaintance, friend,
boyfriend, girlfriend, stranger,
partner, lover
friendship, friendly
to be in love
to make love

6.2   invitations
to invite, invitation
to make an appointment
to join (as in: Will you join us
for lunch?)
to expect (as in: We'll expect
you at six.)
(to) welcome
(to) visit, visitor
to come and see (as in: Why
don't you come and see us
tonight?)

party (as in: We're having a
party tonight.)
to talk
to dance
present (as in: He brought a
present for me.)
guest, host, hostess

6.3   correspondence
(See also 11.1.)
correspondence, to
correspond with ..., to
write (to)
pen friend
letter, registered letter,
express letter
envelope
postcard, picture postcard
(note) paper
sender, addressee
airmail, to send ... by air
pen, fountain, pencil, ball
point/ball pen/biro
india rubber
to receive/to get
(to) answer
by return (of post)

6.4   club membership
club
member, membership
meeting, to meet
subscription
contribution

6.5   government and politics
to govern, government
parliament, member of
parliament
backbencher
opposition
House of Commons, House
of Lords, Lower Chamber,
Upper Chamber
candidate
to elect, election, electorate
vote, to vote
constituency

majority, minority
politics, political
party (as in: Are you a party member?)
names of political parties
e.g. Communist, Conservative, Labour, Liberal, Socialist
right wing, left wing
leader (as in: He is the leader of the opposition.)
(government) department
names of government departments and ministers
e.g. Home Office/Ministry of Home Affairs, Home Secretary/Minister of Home Affairs, Foreign Office/Ministry of Foreign Affairs, Foreign Secretary/Minister of Foreign Affairs, Treasury/Finance Department, Chancellor of the Exchequer/Finance Minister
Prime Minister
(to) reign
king, queen
president
names of titles of the nobility and titles of honour **e.g.** prince, princess, duke, duchess, earl, count, countess, viscount, viscountess, baron, baroness, baronet, knight, dame
nobleman, peer, nobility
knighthood
state (as in: The state owns many factories.)
names of international organisations **e.g.** European Parliament, European Union, European Community, Council of Europe, United Nations/UN, Security Council
Secretary General

6.6   **crime and justice**
crime, to commit a crime
criminal (as in: He is a criminal. He is a member of a criminal organisation.)
accomplice
names of types of criminals
e.g. arsonist, burglar, (drugs) dealer, hijacker, kidnapper, killer, murderer, rapist, robber, terrorist, thief, traitor
names of types of crime **e.g.** arson, burglary, drug traffic, hijacking, kidnapping, to kill, (to) murder, (to) rape, robbery, to rob, to steal, theft, treason
hostage
to shoot, gun
to throw, bomb
victim
to arrest
to interrogate
police, policeman, policewomen, police station
patrol, to patrol
to accuse, accused (as in: The accused refused to answer.)
suspect
culprit
to defend
witness, eyewitness
law, lawyer, lawsuit, lawcourt
judge, jury
solicitor, barrister
public prosecutor
to release, bail
to prove
evidence
guilty
to convict
verdict
sentence (as in: The sentence was five years in prison.)
to sentence

to punish, punishment
prison/jail, prisoner
penalty, death penalty
to appeal
(prison) guard
to escape

6.7   war and peace
peace
disarmament
war, to fight
military service
conscription
conscientious objector
armed forces, army, navy,
air force
soldier
names of military ranks e.g.
officer, general, commander,
colonel, major, captain,
lieutenant, sergeant major,
sergeant, corporal, private
volunteer
civilian
uniform
barracks, headquarters
fortress
hero
enemy, ally
battle
(to) attack
defence, to defend
victory
(to) defeat, to be beaten
negotiations, truce,
armistice, cease-fire, peace
treaty
to shoot, to bomb
weapon
names of types of weapons
e.g. nuclear weapon, bomb,
atomic bomb, gun, pistol,
bullet, missile, grenade
raid
air raid
fall-out, radiation
nuclear war, conventional

war
tank (as in: The enemy tanks
approached the city.)
shelter
spy, to spy, espionage
war correspondent
human rights

6.8   social affairs
(See also 3.2–3.3.)
drugs, hard drugs, soft
drugs, to take drugs
addict
alcohol, alcoholic,
alcoholism
welfare
poverty
equal rights
environment
pollution

7   Health and body care

7.1   parts of the body
names of parts of the body
e.g. arm, back, chest, foot,
hair, hand, head, heart,
kidneys, liver, lungs, neck,
stomach, throat, tooth

7.2   personal comfort
comfortable
(as in: I'm quite comfortable
now. This chair isn't very
comfortable.)
uncomfortable
all right/fine/OK
hunger, hungry; thirst,
thirsty
tired
to rest, rest (as in: What you
need is a good rest.)
to sleep, sleepy
to feel well, to look well

7.3   hygiene
clean, dirty
names of toilet requisites

e.g. brush, comb, razor, scissors, soap, shampoo, toothbrush, toothpaste, sponge, towel
sanitary towel
to shave
to wash (as in: I'd like to wash before dinner. Can you wash these clothes for me?)
to cut (as in: Will you cut my hair, please?)
laundry (as in: Is there a laundry here? Has the laundry come back yet?)

7.4   ailments, accidents
health
ill, to fall ill, to feel ill
to be alive/to live
to die, dead
killed
disease, illness
pain/-ache (as in: I have a headache.)
fever/temperature
to have a cold
dizzy
to feel sick
to hurt
blood, to bleed
bruise, bruised
(un)conscious, to faint, to come to (as in: The patient came to within five minutes.)
to suffer (from)
paralysis, to be paralysed
names of diseases **e.g.** AIDS, brain disease, bronchitis, cancer, cholera, gout, heart disease, infection, inflammation of the lungs, measles, mumps, rheumatism, tuberculosis, typhoid fever, flu
operation, to be operated upon
concussion

to sprain
to cough
sore (as in: I have a sore throat.)
to be overworked
stress
accident, casualty
first aid
to break (as in: He has broken his leg.)
to burn (as in: He has burned his hand.)
to cut (as in: She has cut her finger.)
wound, injury
bandage, dressing, plaster
stitches
stretcher
diet

7.5   medical services
names of medical personnel **e.g.** dentist, doctor/physician, general practitioner/family doctor, specialist, nurse, psychiatrist, surgeon, therapist
names of types of medicine **e.g.** tablet, pill, aspirin, tranquilliser, draught
names of medical institutions **e.g.** clinic, hospital, mental home, surgery
names of types of treatment **e.g.** dental aid/treatment, psychiatric treatment, intensive care, anaesthesia, X-ray, therapy, examination
medicine (as in: Do you take any medicine?)
ambulance
ward (as in: She is in the children's ward.)
patient (as in: The patient is waiting.)

to fill (as in: This tooth was filled a week ago.)
dentures
appointment (as in: What time is your appointment?)
to see a doctor, dentist, etc.
to consult, consultation
to examine
prescription
optician
glasses, contact lenses
fee

7.6   insurance
to insure, insurance
third party insurance
to cover (as in: Does your insurance cover all the damage?)
insurance company, insurance agent
hospital fees, specialists' fees
insurance policy
premium
terms and conditions

....

8   Education

8.1   schooling
education
to learn, to take lessons, a course, etc.
to teach, to train
training
lesson, course, lecture
teacher, master, lecturer, coach, professor, tutor
student, undergraduate, postgraduate
pupil
school, college, institute, academy
names of types of education **e.g.** primary school, secondary school,

university, college, adult education
form (as in: There is an excursion tomorrow for sixth-form pupils.)
homework
timetable
summary, composition, assignment, exercise
exercise book
to make notes
problem (as in: Exercise 1 consists of four mathematical problems.)
term, term-time, semester

8.2   subjects
subject (as in: What subjects did you take at school?)
names of school subjects
e.g. arithmetic, computer science, economics, geography, history, mathematics, physics, reading, science, writing

8.3   qualifications and examinations
diploma, certificate
examination, entrance
examination, final
examination/finals
oral/written
paper (as in: Hand in your papers here.)
multiple choice question, open question
to pass, to fail (examination, test)
result, mark
(in)sufficient
report
level
degree
graduate

9 Shopping

9.1 shopping facilities
shop, to go shopping
market
self-service
names of types of shops
e.g. baker's, butcher's,
department store, DIY,
drugstore, greengrocer's,
grocer's, off-licence,
supermarket, tobacconist's
sale (as in: I've bought this at
the sales.)
to buy, to sell
counter
cash desk
opening hours
retail, wholesale
second-hand
shop window,
window-shopping
(in) stock
it is my (etc.) turn
to show, showcase
to wrap up
to change (as in: I want to
change this shirt; it's not the
right colour.)

9.2 foodstuffs
See 10.1.

9.3 clothes, fashion
(See also General Notions
2.8.1 and 5.1.9.)
clothes
names of clothes e.g.
blouse, coat, dress, hat,
jacket, raincoat, shirt, shoes,
skirt, socks, stockings, suit,
tights, trousers, underwear,
evening wear, evening dress,
jeans
pocket, sleeve
zipper, button, buttonhole
shoelace
belt

fashion
bracelet, earrings, ring,
necklace
jewel, jewellery
purse, wallet
watch (as in: Have you got a
new watch?)
to try on, to put on, to take
off, to wear (clothes)

9.4 smoking
tobacco
pipe, cigar, cigarette
lighter, light (as in: Have you
got a light?)
matches
ashtray
to smoke
no smoking

9.5 household articles
fork, knife, spoon
dish, plate (as in: Mind, the
plates are hot.)
cup, saucer
bottle
bottle opener, tin-opener,
corkscrew
glass, jar, jug
pot, coffee pot, teapot
broom, brush, bucket
crockery
cutlery
duster, dustbin
(to) iron, ironing board
kettle, pan, sieve
string

9.6 prices
(See also General Notions
5.2.1.)
to pay, to spend
money
bargain, reduction,
discount
coins, banknotes
cash, cheque, credit card,
account

bill, receipt
£ (pound)
p (penny, pence)
€ (euro)
names of national
currencies (as required)

....

10   Food and drink

10.1   types of food and drink
(See also General Notions
5.1.6.)
food, meal, snack
to eat, to drink
names of meals e.g.
breakfast, lunch, tea, dinner,
supper
to have breakfast, etc.
course (as in: What's the
main course?)
vegetables
names of vegetables e.g.
beans, cabbage, carrots,
cauliflower, mushrooms,
peas, potatoes, spinach
chips
salad
soup
meat
names of kinds of meat e.g.
beef, lamb, mutton, pork, veal
names of meat products
e.g. hamburger, meatballs,
sausage(s)
fish
names of kinds of fish e.g.
cod, haddock, herring, plaice,
sole, trout
poultry
names of kinds of poultry
e.g. chicken, partridge,
pheasant, turkey
gravy
egg, omelette
cheese
desert, sweet, pudding

ice-cream
vanilla
chocolate (as in: Would you
like a piece of chocolate?
Chocolate ice-cream, please.)
cake, pastry, tart
fruit
names of fruits e.g. apple,
banana, grape, lemon, nut,
orange, raisin, pear,
strawberry, raspberry
cereals
crisps
ice-cubes
spice(s), to spice
names of spices e.g. curry,
garlic, mustard, pepper, salt,
oil, vinegar
flavour
spaghetti, macaroni
flour
bread
slice, piece (as in: Would you
like a piece of cake?)
bread roll
toast, sandwich
bun
pancake
butter
peanut butter, jam
coffee, tea
cream, milk
sugar
drink (as in: Would you like a
drink?)
names of beverages e.g.
beer, fruit juice, mineral
water, soft drinks, orange
juice, water, wine
ways of preparing food e.g.
to bake, to boil, to fry, to grill,
to mix, to peel, to stir
fresh
ingredients

10.2   eating and drinking out
to eat out

snack bar, coffee shop,
restaurant
café, pub, bar, canteen
self-service, help-yourself
to serve, service (as in: No
service in the garden. Service
is included in the bill.)
waiter, waitress
menu, wine
aperitif
to choose
to decide (as in: Have you
decided yet?)
to order
bill
tip, service charge
VAT
to take away (as in: Can I
take this away?)
take-away food
fast food

....

11 Services

11.1 post
(See also 6.3.)
post office, to post, postman
mail
collection
to deliver, delivery
postage
stamp, stamped
letter-box
printed matter
parcel
poste restante

11.2 telephone
(See also 1.3.)
(tele)phone booth/call box
telephone directory
receiver
mobile phone
to make a collect call,
long-distance call
area code
to dial

to ring
engaged, engaged signal
to answer the phone
to hang on (as in: Hang on,
please.)
out of order

11.3 telegraph
telegraph
telegram/wire/cable
word
sender
(to) fax

11.4 bank
(See also 9.6.)
bank
to change (as in: I'd like to
change 500 Swiss francs.)
cheque, travellers' cheque
to cash (as in: I'd like to cash
this cheque.)
(bank) account
to borrow, to lend
interest, rate of interest
to save (as in: I've saved
enough for a trip to
California.)
to put (money) in the bank

11.5 police
See 6.6.
to lose (as in: I've lost my
passport.)
to report (as in: I want to
report a burglary.)

11.6 diplomatic services
consul, consulate
ambassador, embassy
diplomat

11.7 hospital, surgery, etc.
See 7.5.

11.8 garage
garage
trouble, engine trouble
*names of parts of a motor
car* e.g. brake, engine, lights,

headlights, rear lights,
steering, gear, gearbox,
battery, tyre
breakdown
flat tyre
to overheat
dented
windshield
to help
to repair
to tow
to work (as in: My brakes
don't work.**)**

11.9   petrol station
(See also General Notions
2.8.5.)
petrol, fuel, petrol station,
service station
unleaded, leaded
oil, oil change
to check
empty, full

....

12   Places
See 1.2, 5.3 and General
Notions 2.1–2.5.

....

13   Language

13.1   ability, understanding,
expression, correctness
See Language Functions
6.1–6.14 and General

Notions 5.2.7 and 5.2.13.
in addition:
language, dialect, native
language, foreign language
to read, to speak, to
understand, to write
to pronounce,
pronunciation, accent
spelling
fluent, fluency
well (as in: I cannot write
English very well.**)**
a little, not at all
to translate, translation
to interpret, interpreter
dictionary, grammar
sentence, word
idiom
question
clear
to explain
mistake, error, correct,
incorrect
names of languages e.g.
French, German, English,
Spanish, Italian, Dutch,
Swedish, Russian, Arabic,
Chinese, Japanese

....

14   Weather

14.1   climate and weather
See Chapter 7.

Appendix B   Grammatical summary

This summary presents a classified inventory of the grammatical categories, elements and structures which figure as exponents of the functional and notional categories set out in Chapters 5, 6, 7 and 8 and in Appendix A.

The summary is largely identical with Appendix B of *Threshold 1990*, the grammatical content of which is in fact very rich. A learner who is able to exploit fully and freely the lexical and grammatical resources required for the realisation of the range of language functions and, particularly, general notions set out there will have progressed well beyond what is to be expected after two years' part-time study. In progressing from *Threshold* to *Vantage* learners are expanding their range of available language resources largely in the lexical field. In the area of grammar, development is rather in respect of the relaxation of constraints on the use of resources. Many grammatical structures which at *Threshold* level are found only in fixed formulaic expressions will at *Vantage* level be available for more generalised use, leading to greater freedom and flexibility in expression and in understanding. When using those already generalisable at *Threshold* level, *Vantage* level learners will have attained a greater ability to satisfy the criteria of accuracy and fluency. These advances will apply to both speech and writing, though in the nature of things writing, which allows more time for formulation and self-editing, will enable a learner to reflect, to consult works of reference and use a more complex language with greater accuracy. In spoken interaction, where simple, straightforward expression is often more effective than complexity, advances may be more in the greater ability to sustain a longer conversation with freedom and flexibility, and with better adjustment to the nature of the situation and the needs and characteristics of the interlocutor.

For these reasons, the specification of grammatical content in *Vantage* is only marginally different from that of *Threshold 1990*. The main difference lies in the suggestions as to what use learners can be expected to make of their grammatical resources, productively and receptively, in speech and in writing, following the principles set out in the later chapters of the book.

The order of presentation is ascending. That is to say that we first present grammatical information at the word level, classified

according to the traditional parts of speech, with which we expect most users to be familiar. Information is provided concerning the forms of words. Sub-classes are established in terms of the types and functions of words in the major classes set up. Phrases and clauses are then classified according to their formal structure and functional roles in the sentence. Finally, sentences are classified according to their structure and function. At all points cross-reference is made to the relevant sections of Chapters 5 and 6, and Appendix A. The form of reference used is: first the chapter then the section and sub-sections into which the chapter is divided. So, for example, 6.3.2 refers to section 3.2 in Chapter 6. Examples are given, using only vocabulary items which figure as exponents of the functional and notional categories presented in Chapters 5, 6, 7 and Appendix A.
The summary is not conceived as a teaching or reference grammar of English, but simply as a guide to the resources to which a learner has access as a result of learning English to *Vantage* level.

We trust that with a little experience users will find that the systematic presentation of linguistic forms and their function in communication enables reference to be made quickly and efficiently as a further aid to curricular planning and course construction.

A   Word level

A1   Nouns

1.1   Types of noun

1.1.1   proper nouns (written with an initial capital letter)

1.1.1.1   names of days, months, seasons, continents

1.1.1.2   personal and official titles, names of persons, institutions and places, brand names of products, book titles, etc.

These nouns, which are treated as naming unique entities, are indefinite in number and are not specified at *Vantage* level, their relevance to a learner being a matter of personal experience. Learners will be able to recognise or elicit, confirm and store in memory the phonetic form of an unfamiliar proper name as well as to ask for and note down its spelling.

1.1.2   common nouns denoting uncountables

1.1.2.1   abstract, e.g. arts, sports and games (A.4.7), cardinal numbers (6.3.1, 6.4.1, A.1.3), colours (6.5.1.9), points of the compass (6.2.1, 6.2.5)

1.1.2.2   nouns denoting materials, or mass substances, e.g. drinks (A.6.6, A.10.1), foodstuffs (A.10.1), meals (A.3.1, A.5.5, A.10.1), means of transport (A.5.1–2)

1.1.2.3 verbal nouns (gerund) e.g. heating (A.2.5), parking (A.5.3)

1.1.3 common nouns denoting countables: individuals, e.g. family members (A.1.11), job holders (A.1.10), animals (A.7.2.8), plants (A.2.8), objects such as clothes (A.9.3) and household articles (A.9.5), events such as accidents (A.7.4), measures (6.2.8.2 & 4–5)

1.2 **Number (6.4.1)**

1.2.1 regular written plural forms

1.2.1.1 es added to singular form ending:
s address, addresses
x box, boxes
z quiz, quizzes (note -zz-)
sh brush, brushes
ch match, matches
o tomato, tomatoes
(*but* piano, pianos)
(following a consonant only)
y lady, ladies (note i for y)

1.2.1.2 s added to singular form in other cases, including f(e) replaced by ve:
wife, wives
thief, thieves

1.2.2 regular spoken plural forms

1.2.2.1 /ɪz/ added to singular form ending:
/s/ /glɑːs/ /glɑːsɪz/ glass
/z/ /saɪz/ /saɪzɪz/ size
/ʃ/ /dɪʃ/ /dɪʃɪz/ dish
/ʒ/ /gærɑːʒ/ /gærɑːʒɪz/ garage
/tʃ/ /tʃɜːtʃ/ /tʃɜːtʃɪz/ church
/dʒ/ /dʒʌdʒ/ /dʒʌdʒɪz/ judge

1.2.2.2 /s/ added to singular form ending:
/p/ /stɒp/ /stɒps/ stop

/t/ /ædʌlt/ /ædʌlts/ adult
/k/ /bæk/ /bæks/ back
/f/ /lɑːf/ /lɑːfs/ laugh

1.2.2.3 /z/ added to singular form in other cases, including /θ,f/ replaced by /ð,v/:
/bɑːθ/ /bɑːðz/ bath
/naɪf/ /naɪvz/ knife

1.2.3 irregular plural forms:
child, children (A.1.11)
foot, feet (A.7.1)
man, men (A.1.6)
tooth, teeth (A.7.1)
woman, women (A.1.6)
penny, pence (A.9.6)

1.2.4 The following nouns are found in the plural only:
clothes (A.9.3)
means (6.7.3.9)
people (6.8.2)
scissors (A.7.3)
tights (A.9.3)
trousers (A.9.3)

1.2.5 The following nouns are found in the singular only:
information (A.5.1)
luggage (A.5.6)
furniture (A.2.3)
news (A.4.3)

1.2.5.1 uncountable nouns (except in the sense of 'kinds of') (cf. 1.1.2 above):
sugar (A.10.1)
unemployment (A.3.2)

1.3 **Genitive**

1.3.1 forms

1.3.1.1 spoken /z,s,ɪz/ (for use cf. 1.2.2 above) added to:

1.3.1.2 (written), 's:
all singular nouns
the man's head

plural nouns not ending in s
the children's room

1.3.1.3 '(written only; no affix in speech) added to plural nouns ending in s
my aunts' house

1.3.2 Compound nouns

Compound nouns consist of at least two elements, each of which may occur as a separate word. Compound nouns may be written as single words, e.g. newspaper (A.4.9), airport (A.5.1). They may be hyphenated, e.g. waiting-room (A.5.1), ice-cream (A.10.1). In many cases they are written as separate words, often replacing prepositional phrases, e.g. pocket money (A.3.3), insurance company (A.7.6). In all these cases, the first element, which carries the main stress, qualifies the last, the head word. There is considerable uncertainty and inconsistency among native speakers as to the written representation of compound nouns. For instance, 'buttonhole'(A.9.3) may also be found as 'button-hole' and 'button hole'.

1.3.3 Use

At *Vantage* level, learners will regularly use the genitive with nouns denoting persons or animals. In other cases, *of* + NP will normally be used. The learners will be able to understand also such phrases as: a day's work, our country's Prime Minister. Learners should be able to use the genitive to express the possessive relation (6.7.5.1), including ownership, but also other relationships such as parts of the body, kinship, social roles, mental and physical attributes and activities, etc. Mary's feet, John's mother, the secretary's boss, the actor's performance, etc. Learners will recognise and understand compound words, including those they have not previously met, given that they are transparent and composed of words they already know.

A2   Pronouns

2.1   Types of pronoun

2.1.1 demonstrative (5.1.1, 6.8.1.1–2)
this, that, these, those

2.1.2 personal (5.1.1, 6.8.1.1–2)

2.1.2.1 subject forms
I, you, he, she, it, we, they

2.1.2.2 non-subject forms
me, you, him, her, it, us, them

2.1.3 possessive (6.8.1.1–2)
mine, yours, his, hers, ours, theirs

2.1.4 relative (6.8.1.2)
who, whom, which, that

2.1.5 interrogative (5.1.4.7, 6.8.1.1)
who, whom, what, which, whose

2.1.6 reflexive/emphatic (6.8.1.2)
myself, yourself, himself, herself, itself, ourselves, yourselves, themselves

2.1.7 propword (6.8.1.2)
one

2.1.8 indefinite (6.8.2)
somebody, someone,
something; anybody, anyone,
anything; nobody, no-one,
nothing; everybody, everyone,
everything; some, all, any,
none, each, both, it, you

2.2 Gender (3rd person singular only): masculine, feminine, neuter

2.2.2 Use
At *Vantage* level, learners should be able to use the pronouns **he** or **she** corresponding to the sex of the person or animal referred to, using **it** in other cases, e.g. for plants, things and abstracts. They should be aware of the traditional use of **he/him/himself/his** to refer anaphorically to a non-sex-specific personal noun and also of the alternative use of the plural forms, which are not gender-marked.
Good teachers help their students to pass their examinations as against A good teacher helps his students to pass their examinations.
Many people now prefer to use **their**, even after a singular antecedent.
A good teacher will always try to help their students to pass their examinations.

2.2.1 forms
personal pronouns (subject)
he/she/it
(non-subject)
him/her/it
reflexive/emphatic
himself/herself/itself
possessive
his/hers

....

A3 Determiners

3.1 Definite article (5.1.1, 6.8.1.1)

3.1.1 forms
(written) **the**
(spoken) stressed /ðiː/
She is the woman in my life.
unstressed before a
consonant /ðə/
Where's the toilet?
unstressed before a vowel /ði/
What is the EU?

3.1.2 Use
3.1.2.1 with uniques
The sun is shining. (A.14.1)

3.1.2.2 with uniques for a given
person or situation
Send for the doctor. (A.7.5)

3.1.2.3 generically
The cow eats grass and
makes milk. (A.2.8)

3.1.2.4 anaphorically
Italy is beautiful and I like the
country very much.

3.1.2.5 when defined by an adjectival
phrase or clause
the man over there
the woman I saw yesterday

3.2 Indefinite article (6.8.2)

3.2.1 forms
(written)
before consonants a
before vowels an
(spoken)
stressed /eɪ/, /æn/
unstressed /ə/, /ən/

3.2.2   Use

3.2.2.1 for an unspecified person or thing (6.8.2)
There is a man outside.
May I have an orange?

3.2.2.2 to designate frequency (6.3.1.7)
Take the medicine twice a day.

3.2.2.3 to designate amount (6.4.2)
Apples cost 35p a pound.

3.3   Demonstrative (6.8.1.1–2)
this, that, these, those

3.4   Possessive (6.7.5.1, 6.8.1.1–2)
my, your, his, her, its, our, their

3.5   Relative (6.8.1.2)
whose

3.6   Interrogative (6.8.1.1)
what, which, whose

3.7   Quantitative

3.7.1   indefinite (6.4.2)
some, any, no, every, much, many, more, most, several, few

3.7.2   distributive (6.8.2)
each

3.8   Identifying (6.4.1)
another

3.9   Pre-determiners e.g. all (6.4.2)
All the guests have arrived.
such (6.4.3)
He is such a strange man.

3.10   Post-determiners

3.10.1 cardinal numerals (6.4.1)
Who are the three wise men?

3.10.2 ordinal numbers (6.4.1)
She was my first love.

3.10.3 identifying (6.7.4.1) other
The pain is in the other leg.

A 4   Adjectives

4.1   Participial

4.1.1   present, active Vinf + ing
a working mother
This novel is boring.

4.1.2   past, passive Vinf + ed/en
a closed door
My pen is broken.

4.2   Attributive/predicative

4.2.1   attributive only
daily, weekly, main

4.2.2   predicative only
alive, all right, ill, well, so-so

4.2.3   other adjectives are used both attributively and predicatively

4.3   Gradable/non-gradable

4.3.1   non-gradable

4.3.1.1 numerals (6.4.1)

4.3.1.2 material (6.5.1.14)

4.3.1.3 categorial
married/single (A.1.7)
open/closed (6.5.1.12)

4.3.2   gradable

4.3.2.1 polar
old/young (6.5.1.10)
long/short (6.2.8.2)
large/small (6.2.8.1)
wide/narrow (6.2.8.1)

4.3.2.2 neutralised polar
How old is your baby?

4.3.2.3 non-polar
colours (6.5.1.9)
taste (6.5.1.6)
smell (6.5.1.7)

4.4   Comparison of gradable adjectives (6.4.3, 6.7.4.2)

4.4.1 comparative of equality (6.7.4.1)

4.4.1.1 such
Such men are dangerous.

4.4.1.2 like
This tastes like cheese.

4.4.1.3 (the) same (as) (6.7.4.1)
One car is the same as another.

4.4.1.4 as + adj + as (6.7.4.2)
That stone is as sharp as a knife.

4.4.2 comparative of inequality
different (from) (6.7.4.1)
Maltese is different from Italian.
not so + adj + as (6.7.4.2)
Wood is not so heavy as metal.

4.4.3 comparative degree (6.7.4.2)
regular forms

4.4.3.1 (of monosyllabic adjectives)
adj+er
a longer journey

4.4.3.2 (of disyllabic adjectives
with y)
deleting y and adding ier
the heavier suitcase

4.4.3.3 (of some other disyllabics)
adj+er
a quieter room

4.4.3.4 (of other polysyllabic
adjectives) more + adj
a more comfortable chair

4.4.3.5 (of negative adjectives with
un)
more + un+adj
a more unpleasant occupation
alternatively less + positive
adj
a less pleasant occupation

4.4.4 superlative degree (6.7.4.2)
regular forms

4.4.4.1 (of monosyllabic adjectives)
adj+est
the oldest man alive

4.4.4.2 (of disyllabic adjectives
with y)
deleting y and adding iest
the earliest train

4.4.4.3 (of some other disyllabics)
adj+est
the bitterest pill

4.4.4.4 (of other polysyllabic
adjectives)
most + adj
the most useful dictionary

4.4.5 irregular comparatives
**good, better, best, bad, worse,
worst**

4.5 **Complementising adjectives**
(i.e. adjectives regularly
taking particular
complementation structures.
See C2.1.1.4 below.)

4.5.1 of probability (5.2.3.1)
possible, probable

4.5.2 of certainty (5.2.7.1)
certain, sure

4.5.3 of evaluation (6.5.2)
good, bad, wrong

4.5.4 denoting emotional states
(5.2.5)
happy, glad, sorry

4.5.5 denoting moral obligations
(5.2.6.1)
allowed, permitted, free

4.5.6 denoting physical qualities
(6.5.1)
hard, hot, dry

4.5.7 denoting moral qualities
(5.2.6.2–3, 5.3.3.5–6)
kind, nice, good

4.5.8 denoting order (6.3.9)
first, second, next, last

....

A5 Adverbs

5.1 Functions of adverbs

5.1.1 existential (6.1.1)
There is a man at the door.

5.1.2 of time (6.3)
always, already, now, then, ago

5.1.3 place (6.2)
here, there

5.1.4 manner (6.7.3.9)
fast, hard, well

5.1.5 degree (6.4.3)
very, quite, too

5.1.6 direction (6.2.5)
up, down, away

5.1.7 arrangement (6.2.7)
first, last

5.1.8 anteriority (6.3.7)
before, already, yet

5.1.9 posteriority (6.3.8)
afterwards

5.1.10 sequence (6.3.9)
then, next, first, secondly,
lastly

5.1.11 simultaneity (6.3.10)
at the same time

5.1.12 future reference (6.3.11)
soon, tomorrow

5.1.13 present reference (6.3.12)
now, still

5.1.14 past reference (6.3.13)
just, recently

5.1.15 frequency (6.3.17)
always, often, sometimes

5.1.16 intermittence (6.3.19)
sometimes

5.1.17 permanence (6.3.20)
always

5.1.18 repetitiousness (6.3.22)
again

5.1.19 uniqueness (6.3.23)
(only) once

5.1.20 change (6.3.27)
suddenly

5.1.21 preferences (5.2.19–20)
rather ... than

5.2 Form

5.2.1 simple
fast, hard, now, etc.

5.2.2 adj+ly
quickly, certainly, etc.

5.3 Types of adverb

5.3.1 indefinite (6.8.2)
anywhere, everywhere,
somewhere, nowhere, always,
never, sometimes

5.3.2 deictic (6.8.1.1) (and
anaphoric (6.8.1.2))
here, there, now, then

5.3.3 interrogative (6.8.1.1)
relative (6.8.1.2)

5.3.3.1 time
when (?)
When will he come?
I heard him when he left.

5.3.3.2 place
where (?)
Where is my pen?
This is where it is.

5.3.3.3 manner
how (?)
How do you know?
I know how to do it.

5.3.3.4 reason
why (?)
Why did he go?
I know why he went.

5.4   Comparison of gradable adverbs

5.4.1   monosyllabic
fast

5.4.1.1 comparative: adv+er
faster

5.4.1.2 superlative: adv+est
fastest

5.4.2   polysyllabic (adj+ly)
gladly

5.4.2.1 comparative: more + adv
more gladly

5.4.2.2 superlative: most + adv
most gladly
but early, earlier, earliest
(not adj+ly)

5.4.3   irregular comparatives
well, better, best;
badly, worse, worst;
far, further, furthest;
little, less, least

....

A6   Prepositions

6.1   Types

6.1.1   of position (6.2.2)
above, against, among, at,
before, behind, below,
between, in, inside, on,
opposite, outside, over, round,
under, with

6.1.2   distance (6.2.3)
near

6.1.3   direction (6.2.5)
across, along, down, for, from,
into, off, past, through, to,
towards, up

6.1.4   origin (6.2.6)
from

6.1.5   arrangement (6.2.7)
after, before, between, among

6.1.6   time (6.3)

6.1.6.1 point of time (6.3.3)
at, by, in, on

6.1.6.2 duration (6.3.4)
during, for, from ... to,
since, till, until

6.1.6.3 anteriority (6.3.7)
before

6.1.6.4 posteriority (6.3.8)
after

6.1.6.5 future reference (6.3.11)
in

6.1.6.6 frequency (6.3.17)
on

6.1.7   manner (6.7.3.9)
as, by, with

6.1.8   agency (6.7.3.1)
by

6.1.9   instrumentality (6.7.3.4)
with, through

6.1.10 benefaction (6.7.3.5)
for

6.1.11 possession (6.7.5.1)
of, with

6.1.12 inclusion/exclusion (6.7.6.3)
with/without

6.1.13 similarity (6.7.4.2)
as ... as, like

6.2 Use

At *Vantage* level, learners are able to understand and produce the above prepositions in the functions given, together with the phrasal prepositions listed in B6 below, as exponents of the functional and notional categories set out in Chapters 5, 6, 8 and Appendix A. They can extrapolate from those to other transparent uses corresponding to 6.1.1–13, but not to the often arbitrary uses of prepositions in adverbial phrases (e.g. for many reasons), including those in which the choice of preposition is determined by the verb, adjective, etc. qualified (e.g. to look after, to be different from). These they should observe, note, remember, confirm and then use.

....

A7 Verbs

7.1 Forms

7.1.1 Simple forms: regular

7.1.1.1 infinitive: (to +) verb stem
(to) accept, agree, live, try

7.1.1.2 participles:

7.1.1.2.1 present: verb stem (less e after consonant) + ing
accepting, agreeing, living, trying

7.1.1.2.2 past

7.1.1.2.2.a)(written)
verb stem +(e)d
(replacing y by i after consonant)
accepted, agreed, lived, tried

7.1.1.2.2.b)(spoken)
verb stem + /ɪd/ after /t, d/
accepted, ended
verb stem + /t/ after /p, k, f, s, ʃ, tʃ/
hoped, asked, laughed, crossed, danced, mixed, pushed, watched
verb stem + /d/ after all other consonants and all vowels

7.1.1.3 gerund: as present participle

7.1.1.4 finite

7.1.1.4.1 present (6.3.11–12&14)

I/you/we/they accept, agree, live, try
verb stem (+ (e)s in 3rd person singular)
he/she/it accepts, agrees, lives, tries

7.1.1.4.2 past: as past participle

7.1.2 Simple forms: irregular

7.1.2.1 *be*
non-finite a) simple infinitive
be
b) present participle
being
c) past participle
been
d) gerund
being
finite a) unmarked (present)
I am
you/we/they are
he/she/it is
b) past
I/he/she/it was
you/we/they were

7.1.2.2 *have*
non-finite a) simple infinitive
have
b) present participle
having
c) past participle
had
d) gerund
having

finite a) present
I/you/we/they have/'ve
he/she/it has/'s
b) past
had/'d

finite a) present
I/you/we/they do
he/she/it does
b) past
did

7.1.2.3 do
non-finite a) simple infinitive
do
b) present participle
doing
c) past participle
done
d) gerund
doing

7.1.2.4 Modal auxiliary verbs
These have no non-finite
forms, but only unmarked
(present) and past finite
forms, positive and negative:

can	can't	could	couldn't
may	mayn't	might	mightn't
must	mustn't	must	mustn't
shall	shan't	should	shouldn't
will/'ll	won't	would/'d	wouldn't

7.1.2.5 Other irregular verbs differ from regular verbs only in a) the past finite and b) the past participle. The a) infinitive, b) past finite and c) past participle forms for irregular verbs which figure as exponents in the *Vantage* specifications are:

become	became	become	know	knew	known
begin	began	begun	leave	left	left
break	broke	broken	let	let	let
bring	brought	brought	lie	lay	lain
buy	bought	bought	lose	lost	lost
choose	chose	chosen	make	made	made
come	came	come	mean	meant	meant
cost	cost	cost	meet	met	met
cut	cut	cut	pay	paid	paid
draw	drew	drawn	put	put	put
drive	drove	driven	ride	rode	ridden
drink	drank	drunk	ring	rang	rung
eat	ate	eaten	say	said	said
fall	fell	fallen	see	saw	seen
feel	felt	felt	sell	sold	sold
fight	fought	fought	send	sent	sent
find	found	found	shine	shone	shone
fly	flew	flown	shoot	shot	shot
forbid	forbade	forbidden	show	showed	shown
forget	forgot	forgotten	shut	shut	shut
forgive	forgave	forgiven	sing	sang	sung
freeze	froze	frozen	sleep	slept	slept
get	got	got	speak	spoke	spoken
give	gave	given	spend	spent	spent
go	went	gone	stand	stood	stood
hold	held	held	steal	stole	stolen
hurt	hurt	hurt	strike	struck	struck
keep	kept	kept	swim	swam	swum

take	took	taken	understand	understood	understood
teach	taught	taught	undo	undid	undone
tell	told	told	wear	wore	worn
think	thought	thought	win	won	won
throw	threw	thrown	write	wrote	written

At *Vantage* level, learners will confirm, either from the interlocutor or from a reference work, whether verbs they encounter in the course of their reading or listening are regular or irregular and if so what the full verbal paradigm of the verb is.

7.1.3 Compound forms (regular and irregular)

7.1.3.1 perfective
have + past participle

7.1.3.2 progressive (continuous)
be + present participle

7.1.3.3 passive
be + past participle

7.1.3.4 modal auxiliary + infinitive

7.2   **Use**

7.2.1   Types of verb

7.2.1.1 intransitive verbs, denoting:

7.2.1.1.1 actions
dance, play (A.4.4)
talk (A.6.2)

7.2.1.1.2 motion (6.2.4)
come, go, fall, leave, move
follow

7.2.1.1.3 existence (6.1.1)
be, exist, happen (5.1.4.3, 6.1.4)

7.2.1.1.4 weather conditions (A.14.1)
rain, snow

7.2.1.2 transitive (passim)
bring, take, carry, kill
pull, push, put

7.2.1.3 causative (6.7.3.6)
have, get, make

7.2.1.4 inchoative (6.3.27)
become, get, go, turn
fall, start (5.6.12.3, 6.2.4)

7.2.1.5 resultative
win, lose (A.4.7)
qualify, pass (A.3.5)
succeed

7.2.1.6 factitive
make (6.1.1, 6.5.1.14, A.3.1, A.4.6)
cook (A.3.1)

7.2.1.7 complementising verbs (i.e. verbs with clausal, gerundive or infinitival complementation. See B 6.5.1.4 and C 2.1.1.5 below.) denoting:

7.2.1.7.1 cognitive attitudes (5.2.1–2)
think, believe, know
forget, remember, wonder

7.2.1.7.2 volition (5.2.4)
like, want, intend, prefer

7.2.1.7.3 emotions (5.2.5)
love, hate, enjoy, care,
surprise, expect, hope

7.2.1.7.4 commencement (6.3.24)
begin, start

7.2.1.7.5 cessation (6.3.25)
end, stop, finish

7.2.1.7.6 sensory perception (6.5.1.4–7)
watch, hear, see, taste, smell, look

7.2.1.7.7 suasion (6.6.2)
order, tell, request, recommend, invite, forbid, ask, teach

7.2.1.7.8 reflection (6.6.1)
think, believe, hope, know

7.2.1.7.9 expression (6.6.2)
say, answer, ask, tell

7.2.1.7.10 appearance (5.2.2.7.2)
seem, look

7.2.2 Use of verb forms

7.2.2.1 simple present

7.2.2.1.1 general statement without time reference (6.3.14)
Cats and dogs are animals.

7.2.2.1.2 permanently ongoing present actions (6.3.12)
My sister works in a factory.

7.2.2.1.3 habitual actions (6.3.17&22)
I go to bed at 11 p.m. every night.

7.2.2.1.4 future reference with adverbs etc. denoting future time (6.3.11)
The train leaves soon.

7.2.2.1.5 present reference with verbs (cf. A 7.2.4.1 above) denoting: cognitive attitudes (5.2)
I think she is French.
volition (5.2.23–27)
He wants to go to bed.
emotions (5.2.29–44)
I hope the plane will leave on time.
sensory perception (6.5.1.4–7)
This food tastes good.
reflection (6.6.1)
I know you are tired.
appearance (5.2.13)
He seems to be asleep.

7.2.2.2 simple past forms

7.2.2.2.1 verbs denoting actions completed in a past period (6.3.13)
I saw Helen yesterday.

7.2.2.2.2 reporting statements and questions which contained simple present verb forms (5.6.13)
He said dogs and cats were just animals.
He asked if my sister worked in a factory.

7.2.2.2.3 for the equivalents of simple present usage (cf. A 7.7.1 above) but relating to a past period (6.3.13):
general statements
Formerly, there were 240 pence to £1.
permanent states
As a child, I lived in London.
habitual actions
Last year, I drove to work every day.
stative verbs (cf. A 7.7.1.5 above)
He thought it was time to go.

7.2.2.3 present perfect (with reference to the present time)

7.2.2.3.1 anteriority (6.3.7)
Have you seen Mary?

7.2.2.3.2 past reference (6.3.13) i.e. a past action seen as leading to a present condition
He has passed the driving test (implying: he is now qualified to drive).

7.2.2.3.3 continuity (6.3.18) i.e. an action or state, beginning in the past, which is still continuing
I have known Peter for ten years, ever since I met him in Munich.

7.2.2.4 past perfect (with the same denotations as the present perfect, but with reference to a previous time)

7.2.2.4.1 anteriority (6.3.7)
He had met Mary earlier that day.

7.2.2.4.2 past reference (6.3.13)
The guests had arrived.

7.2.2.4.3 continuity (6.3.18)
In 1980, when he died, I had known Peter for ten years.

7.2.2.4.4 in indirect speech (5.6.13), reporting past statements and questions containing present perfect forms
He asked if she had seen Mary lately.
She said the guests had arrived.

7.2.2.5 present continuous

7.2.2.5.1 future reference with verbs of motion (6.3.11)
We are driving to Scotland next week.

7.2.2.5.2 proximal future (6.3.11)
be + going to + infinitive
I am going to sit here all day.

7.2.2.5.3 for present reference i.e. for an action in progress at the time of speaking
Our son is sitting quietly watching television.

7.2.2.5.4 continuity (6.3.18)
It is still raining.

7.2.2.5.5 temporariness (6.3.21) especially with stative verbs (cf. A 7.7.1.5 above)
I am intending to go to France for Easter. (**implying** 'but I may change my mind')

7.2.2.6 past continuous (used with the same denotations as the present continuous, when the frame of reference is the past (6.3.13))

7.2.2.6.1 future motion (6.3.11)
He was driving to Scotland the next day.

7.2.2.6.2 proximal future reference
be + going to + infinitive
He was going to wait a long time.

7.2.2.6.3 action in progress (6.3.18)
She was writing a letter when the telephone rang.

7.2.2.6.4 continuity (6.3.18)
He was still studying to be a lawyer

7.2.2.6.5 temporariness (6.3.21)
The students were working as waiters.

7.2.2.6.6 in indirect speech (5.6.12.1), reporting past statements and questions containing present continuous forms.
He said it was still raining.

7.2.2.7 present perfect continuous

7.2.2.7.1 continuity (6.3.18) in a present frame of reference
I have been standing here since six o'clock.

7.2.2.8 past perfect continuous

7.2.2.8.1 continuity (6.3.18) in a past frame of reference
He had been learning French for ten years and spoke it well.

7.2.2.8.2 in indirect speech (6.3.18), reporting statements and questions containing verbs in the past continuous or present perfect continuous
He said he had been playing tennis (**reporting either** 'I have been playing tennis', **or** 'I was

playing tennis').

7.2.2.9 passive voice (5.3.7.3)

7.2.2.9.1 agentless passive (when the subject of the corresponding active sentence is unknown, irrelevant or not to be revealed), e.g. with the following verbs:
to be allowed (5.2.3.13)
Smoking is not allowed.
to be permitted (5.2.3.13)
Smoking is only permitted in the bar.
to be prohibited (5.2.3.13)
Swimming is prohibited in the river
baked, boiled, fried, grilled (7.10.1)
I prefer my fish to be grilled.
to be included (7.10.2)
Service is included in the bill.
to be seen (6.5.1.4), to be heard (6.5.1.5)
Children should be seen and not heard.
to be called (7.1.1)
The pub in our village is called 'The King's Head'.
to be operated (up)on (7.7.4)
He was operated (up)on for cancer of the stomach.
to be trained (7.8.1)
He was trained as an electronic engineer.
to be stolen
My purse has been stolen.

7.2.2.9.2 The role of subject of a passive verb
a) topicalising the direct object in the corresponding active sentence (6.7.3.2)
The train was delayed by fog.
b) topicalising the indirect object in the corresponding active sentence (6.7.3.3)

I was given another room when I asked for it.

7.2.3   Uses of *be*

7.2.3.1 (as copula) + predicative adjective
John is tired.

7.2.3.2 (as copula) + noun phrase (5.1.1.4)
Mary is a hospital worker.

7.2.3.3 (as copula) + prepositional phrase (6.2.1)
Cornwall is in the West of England.

7.2.3.4 (as copula) + adverb
Our guests are here.

7.2.3.5 existential (6.1)
There are 30 cows on the farm.

7.2.3.6 (+ from) origin (7.1.9)
She is from New Zealand.

7.2.3.7 age (6.5.1.10)
He is six.

7.2.3.8 point of time (6.3.3)
It is 6 p.m.

7.2.3.9 to act a part (7.4.4)
Judi Dench is Lady Macbeth.

7.2.3.10 (perfective aspect + to)
to visit (6.2.1)
She has never been to London.

7.2.3.11 to cost (6.5.2.1)
How much are those trousers?

7.2.3.12 (as auxiliary) + present participle (continuous aspect) (6.3.12, 13)
She is reading a book.

7.2.3.13 (as auxiliary) + past participle (passive voice)
cf. A 7.7.9 below (5.3.7, 6.7.3)
England were defeated by Australia.

7.2.4 Uses of *have*

7.2.4.1 possession, i.e. ownership or the right to use the objects, accommodation, transport, services, etc. (6.7.5.1)
They have a house in the country.

7.2.4.2 attribution, e.g. name (A 1.1)
He has a name I can't pronounce.
address (A.1.2)
They have an address in Mayfair.
telephone number (A.1.3)
We have a new telephone number.
family (A.1.11)
She has four children and six grandchildren.
friends (A.6.1)
We have friends in Strasbourg.
occupation (A.1.10)
salary (A.3.3)
She has a new job and a better salary.
accommodation (A.2.1, 2)
We have a flat in Islington.
pets (A.2.8)
Our daughter has a cat and a dog.
hobbies (A.4.2)
My husband has an unusual hobby.
bank account, etc. (A.11.4)
They say he has a bank account in Switzerland.
qualifications (A.8.3)
My son has a degree in economics.

7.2.4.3 characteristics, e.g. size (6.2.8), shape (6.5.1.1), taste (6.5.1.6), smell (6.5.1.7), colour (6.5.1.9)
Leaves have many different colours, shapes and sizes.

7.2.4.4 part–whole relations
The plane has four engines.
membership of clubs, parties,
etc.(A.4.8, A.6.4–5)
Our club has 2,000 members.

7.2.4.5 to get, receive, e.g. guests (A.5.5), a letter (A.6.3)
We have guests this weekend.

7.2.4.6 to take part in, experience or undergo a process or event, e.g. meals (A.3.1, A.10.1–2)
We had a good meal last night.
toiletry (A.7.3)
You must have a bath or a good wash.
leisure activities, hobbies (A.4)
We are having a party tonight. Do come!
holidays, travel (A.5)
Have a good journey home!
ailments (A.7.4)
She has a bad cold.
operation (A.7.4)
When is she having her operation?
appointments (A.7.5)
Have you an appointment with the doctor?
education (A.8)
She had her education in France.
weather (A.14)
We had a thunderstorm last night.

7.2.4.7 (+ to) obligation (5.2.3.6)
I have to go now.

7.2.4.8 (+ past participle) (perfective aspect) (6.3.7)
They have gone away.

7.2.4.9 (+ NP + infinitive VP) causative (6.7.3.6)
Why not have the garage clean your car?

7.2.4.10 (+ NP + past participle) (causative) (5.3.3.4, 6.7.3.6)
I have my shirts made in Hong Kong.

7.2.5   Uses of _do_

7.2.5.1   perform an action
I always do the washing-up.

7.2.5.2   pro-verb (6.8.1.2)
I am supposed to rest and I do.
(Can I have an apple?) Please do.

7.2.5.3   intensifying (5.1.3)
I do like a good wine!

7.2.5.4   correction (5.1.3)
But I did tell you!

7.2.5.5   negation (5.2.1, 2, 4, etc.)
It doesn't rain in the desert.

7.2.5.6   interrogative (5.1.4)
Do you eat cheese?

7.2.5.7   tag questions (5.2.1.3–4)
You work in an office, don't you?

7.2.5.8   tag responses (5.2.1–2)
Yes, I do. / No, I don't.

7.2.5.9   in special interrogative (5.1.4.6)
Where do you live?

7.2.5.10   strong imperatives and invitations (5.3.10)
Do sit down!

7.2.6   Uses of modal auxiliaries

7.2.6.1   can

7.2.6.1.1   ability, capacity (5.2.9-12) (6.5.2.10)
This actress can sing very well.

7.2.6.1.2   requests (5.3.3.4–5&8)
Can you do this for me?

7.2.6.1.3   offers (5.3.5, 13)
Can I help you?

7.2.6.1.4   permission (5.9–10)
Can I go now?

7.2.6.1.5   possibility (5.2.3.1–3)
It cannot snow in Ghana.

7.2.6.1.6   sensory experience (6.5.1.4–5)
I can see some animals.

7.2.6.2   could

7.2.6.2.1   past of can (6.3.13)
Mithridates could speak many languages.
indirect speech (5.6.12.1)
I said that you could come in.

7.2.6.2.2   tentative offers (5.3.5&13)
Could I be of any help?

7.2.6.2.3   tentative requests (5.3.4–5, 5.6.2&11)
Could you speak more slowly, please?

7.2.6.2.4   suggesting a course of action (5.3.1)
We could go to the cinema.

7.2.6.2.5   giving advice (5.3.6)
You could always ask a policeman the way.

7.2.6.2.6   hypothetical possibility (5.2.3.1)
You could easily get lost if you went on foot.

7.2.6.3   may

7.2.6.3.1   possibility (5.2.3.1–2)
It may rain this afternoon.

7.2.6.3.2   expressing and denying permissibility
Guests may park here.
Visitors may not walk on the lawns.

7.2.6.3.3   asking permission (5.2.3.12&14)
May I drive the car?
including also:
making introductions
May I introduce my husband?
wants and desires (5.2.23)
May I watch television?

asking someone for
something (5.3.14)
May I have a sweet?
interrupting (5.5.14)
May I say something?

7.2.6.4 might

**7.2.6.4.1 suggesting a course of action
(5.3.1)**
We might perhaps go to France.

7.2.6.5 must

**7.2.6.5.1 logical necessity
(5.2.9–12)**
He speaks Flemish and
French. He must be Belgian.

7.2.6.5.2 physical necessity (5.2.11)
We must all die sooner or later.

**7.2.6.5.3 obligation/compulsion
(5.2.15–16)**
You must eat everything on your
plate.

7.2.6.5.4 prohibition (5.2.19)
You must not smoke in here.

7.2.6.5.5 pressing invitations (5.3.10)
You must come and stay with us.

7.2.6.5.6 emphatic statements (5.5.8)
I must stress the fact that our
currency is weak.

7.2.6.6 shall

7.2.6.6.1 future tense (1st person)
I/We shall be in London next
week.

7.2.6.6.2 making an offer
Shall I cook the meal?

**7.2.6.6.3 suggesting a course of action
(5.3.1)**
Shall we go to the theatre?

7.2.6.7 should

7.2.6.7.1 past of shall (6.3.13)
He said it should be done.

7.2.6.7.2 advice (5.3.4)
You should be careful.

7.2.6.7.3 duty (6.5.2.3)
You should do your best.

7.2.6.7.4 expectation
The train should be there by now.

**7.2.6.7.5 rightness, wrongness
(6.5.2.3)**
We should help our mothers.

7.2.6.8 will ('ll)

7.2.6.8.1 future reference (6.3.11)
The sun will rise at 6 a.m.
tomorrow.

7.2.6.8.2 promises (5.2.25)
I will pay you next week.

7.2.6.8.3 requests (5.3.3)
Will you sit down, please.

7.2.6.8.4 invitations (5.3.15)
Will you come to dinner with us?

**7.2.6.8.5 asking if an invitation is
accepted or not (5.3.17)**
Will you visit us, after all?

**7.2.6.8.6 expressing/enquiring about
satisfaction/
dissatisfaction (5.2.5.21–23)**
That will (not) do.

**7.2.6.8.7 confident prediction
(5.2.3.1)**
Tomorrow will be warm and
sunny.

7.2.6.8.8 intentions (5.2.4.4)
I will go to London next week.

7.2.6.8.9 (im)possibility (5.2.3.1–2)
The car won't start.

7.2.6.8.10 capacity (6.5.2.10)
Our car will only run on leaded
petrol.

7.2.6.9 would ('d)

7.2.6.9.1 past of will (6.3.13)
The car wouldn't start.

7.2.6.9.2 indirect speech (5.6.12.1)
He said he would go to London the next day.

7.2.6.9.3 expressing/enquiring about wants/desires (5.2.4.1–3)
What would you like? I'd like an ice-cream, please.

7.2.6.9.4 invitations (5.3.15)
Would you like to come to us for a meal?

7.2.6.9.5 polite requests (5.3.3)
Would you close the window, please?

7.2.6.9.6 hypothetical conditions (6.7.6.8)
If you asked me, I would come.

7.2.6.9.7 unreal conditions (6.7.6.8)
If you had asked me, I would have come.

7.2.6.9.8 advice (5.3.6)
If I were you, I'd go by train.

7.2.6.9.9 preference (5.2.5.19–20)
I'd rather drink coffee than tea.

....

A 8   Conjunctions

8.1   Co-ordinating (joining constituents of equal rank; see C 1 and D 1 below.)

8.1.1   conjunctive (6.7.6.1)

8.1.1.1   and
joining non-contrastive constituents of the same rank
She is always happy and beautiful and she and I are in love and intend to get married.

expressing sequence of actions
He went to the station and took the train to London.

8.1.1.2   but
joining contrastive constituents
He is intelligent but lazy.

8.1.1.3   as well as (non-contrastive)
He is intelligent as well as active.

8.1.1.4   ... as + adjective/verb + as ...
He is as strong as a horse.
He works as hard as he can.

8.1.2   disjunctive (6.7.6.2)

8.1.2.1   or (inclusive)
This play is good for children or older people.

8.1.2.2   or (exclusive)
Are you married or single?

8.2   Subordinating (cf. C 2 below)

8.2.1   complementising that (passim)
I hope that he will come.

8.2.2   temporal (6.3): after (6.3.8), before (6.3.7), since, until (6.3.4), when (6.3.3), while (6.3.10)
He left before I arrived.

8.2.3   spatial (6.2); where (6.2.1), preposition + which
The town where/in which I live is in Dorset.

8.2.4   manner (6.7.3.9): how, how + adverb
Teach me how you make an omelette.
I know how hard you work.

8.2.5   reason, cause (6.7.6.4, 6): as, **because, since**
We are glad because the sun is shining.

8.2.6   effect, consequence (6.7.6.5) **so (+ adj + that)**
It was so hot that I took off my coat. **or** It was hot, so I took off my coat.

8.2.7   conditional (6.7.6.8)
If it doesn't rain, we'll go fishing.

8.2.8   relative (6.8.1.1–2): **what, who, whom, that, which, whose**
What you say interests me.
I know who you mean.

9   Use

At *Vantage* level, learners are able to identify, understand and produce understandably all the words contained in Chapters 5, 6 and 7, and in Appendix A (including the additional vocabulary items they acquire beyond the examples given with regard to the open word classes which are listed in italic sans serif typeface). Learners will also expand their vocabulary autonomously through direct experience of reading and listening. They are able to identify the phonetic form of words they hear (including word stress and the reduction of unstressed vowels) as well as the orthographic form of those they read. They are then able to use reference works to find out the spelling or pronunciation of words they first encounter in the other medium. They know the grammatical classes to which words belong and can use them accordingly.

Learners are aware of the principles of word formation and compounding. They are familiar with common prefixes, such as: *anti-, de-, dis-, non-, pre-, re-, un-,* and suffixes such as: *-able, -hood, -ify, -less, -like, -ness* and can use that awareness to infer the meaning of a word in which one of these affixes is attached to a known word.

B   Phrase level

B1   Noun phrase (NP)

1.1   Form

1.1.1   a pronoun
She loves him.

1.1.2   a noun without determiner

1.1.2.1 proper nouns
Juan lives in Spain.

1.1.2.2 plural indefinites (cf. A 1.2 above)
People are strange.

1.1.2.3 unspecified singular nouns denoting:
colour (6.5.1.9)
red, white and blue
material (6.5.1.14)
I prefer leather to plastic.
days, months (6.3.2, 6.3.3)

Tomorrow is Tuesday the fourth of April.
drinks (7.10.1)
Beer tastes bitter.
foodstuffs (7.10.1)
I don't eat meat.
meals (7.3.1, 7.10.1)
What is for lunch today?
festivals (6.3.3)
Easter is early this year.
numerals (6.4.1)
Three and eight make eleven.
abstracts (7.8)
Education is important.
arts, sports, games (7.4.2)
I prefer music or chess to football.
vehicles seen as means of transport (7.5.1)
I go to London by car or by train.

1.1.3 **determiner + noun (cf. A 3 above)**
Put a stamp on this envelope.

1.1.4 **pre-determiner (cf. A 3.9 above) + determiner + noun**
Did she eat all the cakes?

1.1.5 **(pre-determiner) + determiner + post-determiner (cf. A 3.10 above) + noun**
Is this your first visit to Britain?

1.1.6 **(pre-determiner +) (determiner +) (post-determiner +) adjective(s) + noun**
She was wearing a nice new white dress.

1.1.6.1 **order of adjectives: quality + size + shape + colour + material**
What happened to all those nice little dark blue woollen dresses?

1.1.7 **(determiner +) adverb of degree (6.4.3) + adjective + noun**
Chess is a very different game.

1.1.8 **(determiner +) qualifying adverb + adjective + noun**
He is a happily married man.

1.1.9 **(determiner +) (adverb +) (adjective +) noun + relative adjunct**

1.1.9.1 **adverb**
Do you know the way back?

1.1.9.2 **prepositional phrase**
The chair in the bedroom is broken.

1.1.9.3 **to + infinitive verb phrase (VPinf)**
I need a clean shirt to wear.

1.1.10 **(determiner +) (adverb +) (adjective +) noun + relative clause**
Jane, I'd like you to meet a very nice young man I know.

1.1.11 **NP denoting container (6.4.2) or measure (6.2.8.2 & 4–5, 6.4.2) + of + NP denoting mass substances, materials or plurals**
I'd like a pound of apples and a large bottle of dry white wine.

1.1.12 **nominalised verb phrases (VPs)**

1.1.12.1 **to + VP infinitive**
I want to go home.

1.1.12.2 *wh* + **to + VP infinitive**
I don't know what to do.

1.1.12.3 **VP gerund**
I like swimming in the sea.

1.1.13 **use of nominalised verb phrases**

1.1.13.1 **to + infinitive**

1.1.13.1.1 **as subject**
To kill people is wrong.

1.1.13.1.2 **following complementising adjectives (cf. A 4.5 above) of probability (5.2.9, 10)**
It is likely to rain tomorrow.

of certainty (5.2.13–14)
He is expected to arrive late.
of evaluation (6.5.2)
It is wrong to kill people.
denoting emotional states
(5.2.29–50)
I am glad to see you.
denoting physical qualities
(6.5.1)
This bed is soft to lie on.
denoting moral qualities
(5.2.49)
It is kind of you to invite us.
denoting order (6.3.9)
They are always the last to arrive.
denoting availability (6.1.3)
Is the food ready to eat?

**1.1.13.1.3 with adjectives and adverbs
of degree (6.4.3)
enough**
The tea is now cool enough to
drink.
Have you had enough to eat?
too
My grandfather is too old to
travel.
very
This case is very heavy to carry.

**1.1.13.1.4 following certain
complementising
verbs (cf. A 7.1.7 above)
forget, remember**
Did you remember to close the
window?
verbs of volition (5.2.23–27)
I want to become a doctor.
**verbs expressing emotions
(5.2.29–46)**
I hope to pass the examination.
commencement (6.3.24)
It is beginning to rain.
suasion (6.6.2)
Tell him to come here.
appearance (5.2.13)
She seems to be asleep.

**1.1.13.1.5 following an indefinite
pronoun (6.8.2)**
I want something to eat.

**1.1.13.1.6 following an indefinite
adverb (6.8.2)**
I have nowhere to sleep.

1.1.13.2 *wh* + to + VP infinitive

**1.1.13.2.1 following certain
complementising adjectives
certain (5.2.13)**
Are you certain where to go?

**1.1.13.2.2 following certain
complementising verbs
denoting cognitive attitudes
(5.2) tell, teach**
Do you know where to go?
Teach me how to swim.

1.1.13.3 VP gerund

1.1.13.3.1 as subject
Swimming in the sea can be
dangerous.

**1.1.13.3.2 following certain
complementising verbs
forget, remember (5.2.7–8)**
I'll never forget meeting the
Prime Minister.
like, intend, prefer (5.2.23–28)
She prefers driving to going by
train.
love, hate, enjoy (5.2.32–34)
I quite enjoy travelling by air.
stop, finish (6.3.25)
At last it has stopped raining.

1.1.13.3.3 in prepositional phrases
I don't believe in punishing little
children.
Don't leave without paying the
bill.

1.2   Use of noun phrases

1.2.1   functions of noun phrases

1.2.1.1 as subject (6.7.3.1–3)
The young woman ran away.

1.2.1.2 as direct object of transitive verb (6.7.3.2)
We won the football match.

1.2.1.3 as indirect object of verb of giving (6.7.3.3)
I gave my sister a CD player.

1.2.1.4 in prepositional phrases
We went to a fine old house.

1.3 Use

At *Vantage* level, learners are able to use all the types of noun phrase shown above, productively as well as receptively. They may be expected to produce them creatively in speech, however, only in relatively simple form, with not more than, say, three qualifying elements in addition to the basic determiner structures + noun. In writing, they will be constrained by stylistic rather than grammatical considerations.

....

B2 Adjective phrases

2.1 Forms

2.1.1 predicative adjective + post-modifier
This food is not good enough.

2.1.2 predicative adjective + adjunct
Smoking is bad for you.

2.1.3 predicative complementising adjective + complement phrase or clause (cf. C 2.1.1.1 below)
Apples are good to eat.
It is probable that he will come.

2.1.4 adverb of degree (6.4.3)+ gradable adjective
She is a very beautiful and most intelligent woman.

2.1.5 adverb + past participle
This is a very poorly made dress.

2.2 Use

At *Vantage* level, learners are able to recognise and produce all the above types of adjectival phrase.

....

B3 Pronoun phrase

3.1 Forms

3.1.1 determiner + adjective + one(s) (6.8.1.2)
Give me the largest one(s).

3.1.2 some + of + determiner + mass noun/plural noun
I'd like some of the butter, please.

3.1.3 indefinite pronoun (6.8.2) + adjunct
May I have something to drink?

3.1.4 indefinite pronoun + adjective
He told me nothing new or interesting.

3.1.5 indefinite pronoun + relative clause
Susan is someone I met in Spain.

3.2   Use

At *Vantage* level, learners should be able to understand and produce the above types of pronominal phrase in speech and writing.

....

B4   Verb phrase (VP)

4.1   Forms containing one main verb

4.1.1   intransitive verb (6.2.4)
The train arrived.

4.1.2   copula + NP complement (5.1.1)
This animal is a dog.

4.1.3   transitive verb + NP direct object (6.7.3.2)
I saw a bird.

4.1.4   transitive verb + NP direct object (6.7.3.2) + NP indirect object (6.7.3.3)
I showed the letter to his mother.
(+ benefactive 6.7.3.5)
I gave John the letter for Marion.
(+ instrumental 6.7.3.4)
Susan opened the door for me with her key.

4.1.5   adverb + verb
He and I always agree.

4.1.6   verb + adverb(s)
He walked home again very slowly afterwards.

4.1.7   copula + adjective phrase
She is very intelligent.

4.1.8   copula + adverb
The fork is here.

4.1.9   copula + prepositional phrase
The cup is on the table.

4.1.10   stative verb + complement NP
She seems a nice girl.

4.1.11   stative verb + adjectival phrase
The fish tastes very nice.

4.1.12   verb + adverbial (prepositional) adjunct
Our guests sleep in this bedroom.

4.1.13   phrasal verbs: verb + adverbial particle (+ NP)
What did the wind blow down?
The wind blew down the tree.
The wind blew the tree down.
The wind blew it down.
The tree blew down.
Note This construction is distinct from:
verb + preposition (+ NP), which it resembles
What did the wind blow down?
The wind blew down the valley.
The wind blew very hard down the valley.
The wind blew down it very hard.

4.2   Short answers (5.1.5, 5.2.1) auxiliary or pro-verb only

4.2.1   *be*
(Are you French?) Yes, I am.

4.2.2   *have*
(Has he finished?) Yes, he has.

4.2.3   modals
(Can I go now?) Yes, you can.

4.2.4   *do*
(Do they like mutton?) No, they don't.

4.3   Pro-verb phrase do so

He asked me to stop and I did so.

4.4 Use

Learners at *Vantage* level should be able to understand the verb phrases listed above and to use them productively as exponents of the functional and notional categories set out in Chapters 5, 6 and 7. In principle, the verb phrase comprises everything in a sentence apart from the subject NP and is capable of very great complexity. In respect of the verb forms themselves, well over 100 combinations of a main verb with its auxiliary verbs are possible. Furthermore, the nominal and adverbial constituents of a verb phrase may be of indefinite complexity. The ability of learners to process such complex syntactic structures receptively is limited and their ability to produce them very much more so. In progressing from *Threshold* to *Vantage*, these constraints are much reduced, especially in reading and writing when not under strong time pressures and when reference materials can be consulted. In spoken interaction, a learner at *Vantage* level will be able, as a listener, to identify the verb forms used by the interlocutor(s) and to understand most verb phrases, using compensation strategies (see Chapter 12) where necessary. As a speaker, a *Vantage* learner is recommended to aim at accuracy and fluency in the use of relatively simple sentences, rather than longer and more complex sentences.

B5 Adverb phrase

5.1 adverb of degree (6.4.3) and gradable adverb
He drove very fast.

5.2 comparative of equality/

inequality (6.7.4.2)
He did as well as he could.

5.3 prepositional phrase(s) (6.2.2–7, 6.3.3–4&7–8, 6.7.6.9) preposition + NP
We went to the seaside last week by train.

5.4 Use

At *Vantage* level, learners are able to identify, understand and produce adverbial phrases as above, including prepositional phrases in the functions given in Chapter 6.

B6 Preposition phrase

Note We mean by this a phrase fulfilling the function of a preposition, not an adverbial consisting of a preposition + a noun phrase, often termed a prepositional phrase. (4.1.12)

6.1 Preposition + NP + of

6.1.1 in front of (6.2.2)
The bus stop is in front of the bank.

6.1.2 in the centre of (6.2.2)
The cathedral is in the centre of the city.

6.1.3 **at the back of (7.4.4)**
The plates are at the back of the cupboard.

6.1.4 **at/to the side of (6.2.2)**
Put the knife to the side of the plate.

6.1.5 **at the end of (6.2.2)**
Their house is at the end of the road.

6.1.6 **to the left/right of (6.2.5)**
The fridge is to the right of the washing-machine.

6.1.7 **in the neighbourhood of (6.2.3)**
Sonning is in the neighbourhood of Reading.

6.2 **Adverb and preposition**

6.2.1 **next to (6.2.2)**
We live next to an actor.

6.2.2 **far (away) from (6.2.3)**
The house is not far from the shops.

6.2.3 **out of (6.2.6)**
An animal came out of the forest.

C   Clause level

C 1   Clause types and functions

1.1 **Main clause (NP and finite VP)**

1.1.1 as sole constituent of a simple sentence (See D 1.1 below.)
I will come home soon.

1.1.2 as co-ordinate constituent of a compound sentence
My work is nearly finished and I will come home soon.

1.1.3 as main clause in a complex sentence
I will come home when my work is finished.

1.2 **Subordinate clause**

1.2.1 as short answer to a *wh*-question
(When are you coming home?)
When my work is finished.

1.2.2 as part of a complex sentence
I left when my work was finished.

C 2   Forms and functions of subordinate clauses

2.1 **Noun clauses**

2.1.1 **(that) + NP + VP finite**

2.1.1.1 following it + *be* + adjective of probability (5.2.3.1–2)
It is likely that it will snow tonight.
certainty (5.2.13–14)
It is expected that the teachers will strike.
evaluation (6.5.2)
It is good that he has come.

2.1.1.2 following it + certain other complementising verbs e.g. **surprise** (5.2.5.30)
It surprises me that he has left already.

2.1.1.3 following it + *be* + certain noun phrases (e.g. 5.2.5.6)
It is a pity (that) they cannot come.

2.1.1.4 following certain complementising adjectives (cf. A 4.5 above)
certainty (5.2.2.7.1–2)
I am sure (that) he will come.
denoting emotional states (5.2.5)

I am sorry (that) she is ill.
expressing surprise (5.2.5.30)
I am surprised (that) he loves
her.

**2.1.1.5 following certain
complementising verbs
(cf. A 7.1.7 above)
reporting (5.1.1.2)**
He said that the food was very
good.
knowing (5.2.2.1–3)
I know (that) she works in an
office.
remembering (5.2.2.4–5)
I remember (that) he is very tall.
expressing certainty (5.2.2.7)
Do you think (that) it will be
foggy?
expressing hope (5.2.5.8)
I do hope (that) you will come to
dinner.

2.1.2 if + NP + VP finite

**2.1.2.1 in indirect questions,
following verbs of:
asking (5.1.2)**
She asked if he was ready yet.
wondering (5.2.2.7.3, 5.3.3.5)
I wonder if you could help me.
knowing (5.2.2.1–2)
I don't know if you will like
this.

2.1.3 wh clause (wh + NP + VP)

2.1.3.1 as subject
What I like is watching
football.

2.1.3.2 as complement after be
This is not what I expected or
wanted.

**2.1.3.3 in indirect questions,
following verbs of:
asking (5.1.2.)**
I asked him where he was going.
wondering (5.2.2.7.3)

I wonder where my keys are.
telling (5.1.2)
I told him when the train was
leaving.
remembering (5.2.2.4–6)
I have forgotten when he was
born.
knowing (5.2.2.1–3)
I don't know why he left her.

2.1.4 what + VP

2.1.4.1 as subject
What interests me is politics.

2.1.4.2 as object
I know what is meant.

2.1.5 NP + VP infinitive

**2.1.5.1 following verbs of sensory
perception**
I saw him drive away.

2.1.5.2 following causative have
I had the laundry clean my
raincoat.

2.1.6 NP + to + VP infinitive

**2.1.6.1 following verbs of volition
(5.2.4)**
I want my son to become a
doctor.
liking (5.2.5.16–18)
I do not like my children to
smoke.
suasion (5.3.3)
Tell that man not to smoke in
here.
cognition (5.2.2.1–3)
I know him to be a kind man.

2.1.7 NP + VP gerund

**2.1.7.1 following verbs of
remembering (5.2.2.4–6)**
I remember my brother being
born.

liking and disliking
(5.2.5.16–18)
I hate insects eating my
vegetables.

2.1.8   NP (+ to be) + adjective
I prefer water (to be) boiled.

2.1.9   pro-clause so

2.1.9.1 following certain
complementising verbs
of reflection (6.6.1)
(Will he come?) I hope/think/
believe so.
of expression (6.6.2)
(Is she really French?) She says
so.

2.2   **Adjectival (relative) clauses**

2.2.1   following NP human

2.2.1.1 who + VP
This is the man who lives with
me.

2.2.1.2 that + VP
This is the woman that defeated
me at chess.

2.2.1.3 whom + NP + VP
Alison is the girl whom I met in
Turkey.

2.2.1.4 (that) + NP + VP
She is the actress (that) I like
best.

2.2.1.5 preposition + whom + NP
+ VP
Mrs Smith is a lady with whom I
work.

2.2.1.6 (who/that) + NP + VP +
preposition
Joe's a man (who/that) I play
rugby with.

2.2.1.7 (possessive) whose + NP + VP
The man whose daughter taught
me French has just died.

2.2.1.8 whose + NP + NP + VP
This is a colleague whose wife I
trained as a nurse.

2.2.2   following NP non-human

2.2.2.1 which/that + VP
I read a book which/that
explains nuclear physics.

2.2.2.2 which/that + NP + VP
Have you seen the car which/that
I bought?

2.2.3   following superlative

2.2.3.1 (that) NP + VP
Is that the best (that) you can
do?

2.2.4   restrictive and non-restrictive
relative clauses

2.2.4.1 restrictive (Note absence of
comma in the written form
and a single tone-group in
speech.)
I 'do not buy ·books which are
ˌboring. (i.e. I only buy
interesting books.)

2.2.4.2 non-restrictive (Note presence
of comma in the written form
and separate tone-group for
the relative clause in speech.)
I 'do not ˅buy ·books, | which are
ˌboring. (i.e. I do not buy any
books, because all books are
boring.)

2.3   **Adverbial clauses**

2.3.1   of place (6.2)

2.3.1.1 where . . . (6.2.2)
It hurts where I put my finger.

2.3.2   of time (6.3), denoting

2.3.2.1 point of time (6.3.3, 6.3.10)
when
Please come when I call you.

2.3.2.2 duration (past) (6.3.4) **since**
It is quiet here since Ian left.

2.3.2.3 duration (future) (6.3.4, 6.3.25) **until /till**
I will (not) sleep until/till he returns.

2.3.2.4 anteriority (6.3.8) **before**
The accident happened before I arrived.

2.3.2.5 posteriority (6.3.8) **after**
After we finished eating, we paid the bill.

2.3.2.6 simultaneity (at point in time) (6.3.10) **as soon as**
Tell me as soon as the boat sails.

2.3.2.7 simultaneity (duration) (6.3.10) **while**
There will be a short delay while we check the plane.

2.3.3 expressing logical relations (6.7)

2.3.3.1 reason, cause (6.7.6.4) **because**
I eat brown bread because it is good for me.

2.3.3.2 cause (6.7.6.4) **as**
As he was tired, he lost the match.

2.3.3.3 reason (6.7.6.6) **since**
Since you are sorry, I'll forgive you.

2.3.3.4 effect (6.7.6.5) **so**
He turned right, so he lost his way.

2.3.3.5 effect (6.7.6.5) **so ... (that)**
The suitcase was so heavy (that) I couldn't carry it.

2.3.3.6 condition (6.7.6.8) **if**
(See also 5.3.4.2)
If you like, you can come too.

2.3.3.7 comparison (6.7.4.2) **than**
The tea is stronger than I had expected.

as ... as
He works as hard as he can.

not so ... as
He is not so intelligent as he thinks he is.

....

3   Use

At *Vantage* level, a learner is able to recognise and produce all the above clause types, and to use them as appropriate in the functions set out in Chapters 5, 6 and 8, provided that the constituents of the clause are not excessively numerous or complex (e.g. by the 'nesting' of further clauses and phrases, as in: '*The couple we met last year in that delightful little village in the South of France we stayed in overnight on our way from Nice to Valence – or was it Orange, I always get the two places confused – I am sure were in that car we just overtook.*'). Whilst such sentences are not infrequent in conversation between native speakers who know each other well, the memory load upon a *Vantage* learner as a result of this degree of separation between the subject and predicate of a main clause is excessive. More appropriate would be: '*Do you remember that delightful little village we stayed in overnight in the South of France? It was when we were on our way from Nice to Valence. Or was it Orange? I often get the two places confused. Well, I'm sure that couple we met there were in that car we just overtook.*'

D   Sentence level

....

D1   Form

1.1   **Simple sentences, consisting of one main clause (cf. C1.1.1 above)**

1.2   **Compound sentences, consisting of two or more main clauses, linked by co-ordinating conjunctions (cf. A 8.1 above)**

1.3   **Complex sentences, consisting of a main clause + one or more subordinate clauses (cf. C1.2 above)**

....

D2   Sentence types

2.1   **Declarative**

2.1.1   affirmative (5.1.2)
The tourists ate their sandwiches.

2.1.1.1   emphatic affirmative (5.1.3, 5.2.2.7.1)
NP + *do* + VP infinitive
I did tell you.

2.1.2   negative

2.1.2.1   NP + *be/have* + not/n't + ...
It isn't cold in Africa.

2.1.2.2   NP + *do*/modal + n't + VP infinitive
It doesn't rain in the Sahara Desert.
He can't speak French.

2.1.2.3   with negative indefinite pronouns, adverbs, etc. (6.8.2)
Nobody likes me.
Old soldiers never die.

2.1.2.4   use of negative expression + indefinite pronoun, adverb, etc.
He won't eat anything.
Nobody is safe anywhere.

2.2   **Interrogative**

2.2.1   decision (yes/no) questions

2.2.1.1   *be/have* (+ not) + NP + ...
Are you ready?
Haven't you been to Italy?

2.2.1.2   *do*/modal (+ not) + NP + infinitive
Don't you eat meat?
Can I help you?

2.2.1.3   declarative sentence with high-rising intonation
You're ˈready?

2.2.1.4   affirmative sentence + negative tag question with falling intonation, conducive to the answer 'yes'
You ˈare ˇcoming, | ˌaren't you?
with low-rising intonation, non-conducive
You are ˌGerman, | ˌaren't you?

2.2.1.5   negative sentence + positive tag with falling intonation conducive to the answer 'no'
You ˈdon't aˇgree with her, | ˌdo you?
with low-rising intonation, non-conducive
Jane ˈhasn't ˌleft yet, | ˌhas she?

2.2.2   special questions (*wh*) requiring an answer consisting in or containing:

2.2.2.1   a subject NP (human)
Who + VP finite
Who has drunk my tea?
(Sorry, I have.)

2.2.2.2 a subject NP (non-human)
What + VP finite
What interests you most?
(Politics.)

2.2.2.3 specification of a subject NP
Which + NP + VP finite
Which driver owns this car? (Me.)

2.2.2.4 an object NP (human)
Who/Whom + auxiliary + NP +
VP non-finite, containing a
transitive verb
Who did you see last night?
Whom did you see last
night?

2.2.2.5 an object NP (non-human)
What + auxiliary + NP + VP
non-finite containing a
transitive verb
What do you want for breakfast?

2.2.2.6 a specified object NP
Which + NP + auxiliary + NP +
VP non-finite, containing a
transitive verb
Which sport do you like best?

2.2.2.7 an adverbial of time
When + interrogative
sentence structure
When does the train leave?

2.2.2.8 an adverbial of place
Where + interrogative
sentence structure
Where did you go afterwards?

2.2.2.9 an adverbial of manner
How + interrogative sentence
structure
How can I pay the bill?

2.2.2.10 an adverbial of reason
(or relative declarative
sentence)
Why + auxiliary +
interrogative sentence
Why do you go to church?
(Because I believe in God.)

Why are you afraid of the police?
(I don't know, but . . .)

2.3 Imperative

2.3.1 VP infinitive
Go to bed at once.

2.3.2 **you** + VP infinitive
John, you be a good boy and eat
your spinach!

2.3.3 **do** + VP infinitive
Do please sit down!

2.3.4 **let's** + VP infinitive
Let's go to the theatre!

D 3 Functions of sentence types

3.1 Affirmative sentences

3.1.1 reporting (5.1.2)

3.1.1.1 narrating an event (5.1.2)
The flight arrived at 9 a.m.

3.1.1.2 describing (5.1.2)
Sue has blue eyes.

3.1.2 answering questions (5.1.5)
It happened early this morning.

3.1.3 making statements
concerning:

3.1.3.1 agreement (5.2.1.1–2)
I quite agree with you.

3.1.3.2 knowledge (5.2.2.1–3)
I know he was here yesterday.

3.1.3.3 memory (5.2.2.4–6)
I remember meeting you in 1985.

3.1.3.4 probability (5.2.3.1–2)
I am likely to see him in London.

3.1.3.5 logical necessity (5.2.3.3–5)
Casa Vecchia must be in Italy.

3.1.3.6 certainty (5.2.2.7)
I am sure he will come.

3.1.3.7 obligation (5.2.3.6–8)
You must stay here till I
return.

3.1.3.8 ability (5.2.3.9–11)
All young Swedes can speak
English.

3.1.3.9 permissibility (5.2.3.12–14)
Parking is allowed from
6 p.m. to 8 a.m.

3.1.4   expressing:

3.1.4.1 wants and desires (5.2.4.1–3)
I want to see my friend.

3.1.4.2 intentions (5.2.4.4–6)
I am going to buy a new car.

3.1.4.3 preference (5.2.5.19–20)
I'd rather die than give up
tennis.

3.1.4.4 pleasure, happiness (5.2.5.1)
I'm delighted to see you again.

**3.1.4.5 displeasure, unhappiness
(5.2.5.2)**
I'm feeling very miserable this
morning.

3.1.4.6 liking (5.2.5.16)
I like cakes and pastries very
much.

3.1.4.7 dislike (5.2.17)
This coffee tastes horrible.

3.1.4.8 satisfaction (5.2.5.21)
This brandy is just what I need.

3.1.4.9 dissatisfaction (5.2.5.22)
The shower in the bathroom is
not working.

3.1.4.10 interest (5.2.5.28)
I am very interested in old
buildings.

3.1.4.11 lack of interest (5.2.5.29)
I don't care if it rains all day.

3.1.4.12 surprise (5.2.5.30)
I'm surprised he didn't phone.

3.1.4.13 hope (5.2.5.8)
I hope to become an actress.

3.1.4.14 fear (5.2.5.10)
I'm afraid of the dark.

3.1.4.15 gratitude (5.2.5.36)
I'm very grateful to you for
helping me.

3.1.4.16 moral obligation (5.2.6.1)
You should be kind to animals.

3.1.4.17 regret (5.2.5.6)
I'm very sorry that I broke your
window.

3.1.4.18 sympathy (5.2.5.6)
I'm so sorry to hear your wife
is ill.

3.1.5   giving:

3.1.5.1 suggestions (5.3.1)
We might perhaps go to Turkey
this year.

3.1.5.2 advice (5.3.6)
You ought to see a doctor.

3.1.5.3 warning (5.3.7)
This plate is very hot.

3.1.5.4 instructions (5.3.3.2)
You cut the paper like this.

3.1.5.5 directions (5.3.3.2)
The party will meet outside the
hotel at 5.30 a.m.

3.1.6   structuring discourse by:

3.1.6.1 introducing a theme (5.5.2)
I'd like to say something about
world poverty.

3.1.6.2 expressing an opinion (5.5.3)
In my opinion, nuclear weapons
are useless.

3.1.6.3 giving emphasis (5.5.6)
I must stress the fact that we are friends.

3.1.6.4 repeating what one has said (5.6.12.1)
I said that I wanted a drink, please.

3.2 Emphatic affirmative sentences

3.2.1 correcting a negative statement (5.1.3.2)
But I did see him!

3.2.2 expressing certainty (5.2.7.1)
I'm sure he does eat cheese.

3.2.3 expressing strong positive feelings
I do like ice-cream!

3.3 Negative sentences

3.3.1 correcting a positive statement (5.1.3.1)
No, I didn't see her.

3.3.2 denying statements (5.2.1.6)
But I know nothing about it.

3.3.3 denying knowledge, belief, etc. (5.2.2.1, etc.)
I don't think so.

3.3.4 expressing negative feelings and attitudes (5.2.5.17, etc.)
I don't like hot milk.

3.3.5 withholding permission (5.3.11–12)
You cannot go out tonight.

3.4 Decision questions

3.4.1 asking for confirmation (5.1.4.1–5)
You won, didn't you?

3.4.2 enquiring about:

3.4.2.1 agreement (5.2.1.3)
Don't you think that's dangerous?

3.4.2.2 knowledge (5.2.2.2)
Do you know my cousin?

3.4.2.3 memory (5.2.2.5)
Do you remember the war?

3.4.2.4 probability (5.2.3.2)
Are you likely to vote Labour?

3.4.2.5 necessity (5.2.3.5)
Must you leave already?

3.4.2.6 certainty (5.2.2.7.6)
Are you sure it has stopped raining? Do you really think so?

3.4.2.7 ability (5.2.3.1)
Are you able to see?

3.4.2.8 permissibility (5.2.3.14)
Is it all right if I open the window?

3.4.2.9 wants, desires (5.2.4.3)
Would you like to dance?

3.4.2.10 intentions (5.2.4.6)
Are you thinking of getting up?

3.4.2.11 preferences (5.2.5.20)
Do you prefer orange juice to beer?

3.4.2.12 feelings (5.2.5)
Do you like my new hat?

3.4.3 making requests (5.3.3)
Could you open the window, please?

3.4.4 asking for help (5.3.3.8)
Can you help me, please?

3.4.5 offering assistance (5.3.13)
Can I help you?

3.5 Special (*wh*) questions

3.5.1 asking for specific information (5.1.3)
How far is it to the station?

D 4   Use

At *Vantage* level, learners are able to understand and produce simple, compound and complex sentences within the limits of the *Vantage* specification, given that noun and verb phrases are not overloaded (cf. D 1.3 and B 4.6 above). In speech, they can produce complex sentences which are straightforward in character, e.g. limited to one or two subordinate clauses of relatively simple structure with a main clause frame of a basic character, as for instance in the examples in this summary. Learners are able to understand complex sentences containing more than one embedded clause, given that the internal structure of clauses and the relations between them are not unduly complicated. It is difficult to define exact limits. Any learner who has attained *Vantage* competence should have little difficulty with such sentences as

He says he wants to leave as early as possible tomorrow morning.
When I left, I saw that it was starting to rain, and so I decided to put on my raincoat

or even:
We thought you must be ill because you didn't arrive for the meeting and when we left you earlier you'd said you had a headache.

A *Vantage* reader will be able to handle written textual material of greater complexity, given that it does not require specialist knowledge. Listening comprehension is more demanding and the chain of understanding may be broken if the speech presented under conditions where repair strategies cannot be used is too complicated or too dense. In writing, simplicity is generally a virtue. In conversation, learners are able to understand the interlocutor's contributions within the limits of this specification. Where that is not the case, they are able to operate repair strategies as set out in Chapter 12. Their own contributions may be expected to be relatively short, but relevant, appropriate, fluent and accurate. As specified in Chapter 8, they are also able to produce extended, well-formed discourse to report events, describe people and things and express ideas at greater length in speech as well as in writing.

Appendix C   Pronunciation and intonation

Pronunciation

Communication depends upon mutual intelligibility. That is to say that it is only possible if the language forms produced by the speaker are identified and understood by the listener. It is therefore the responsibility of speakers to pronounce them as *intelligibly* as possible, and it is also the responsibility of listeners actively to seek to identify what has been said and to use appropriate repair procedures if they are unable to do so. The ease of communication depends largely on the extent to which speaker and listener share a common practice. Speakers of the same dialect understand each other without difficulty, but widely separated dialects may well be mutually unintelligible. For purposes of national (or international) communication standard languages with standard pronunciations have generally developed, based usually on the speech of educated people in capital cities, or that of some other prestigious social group. The standard language is widely used in the education system, in the serious media and in middle-class life and culture. This is not to say that all users of a standard pronunciation sound alike. The speaker's socio-regional provenance may be clearly marked and easily detectable by an experienced listener. It may well be important to the individual's sense of identity that this should be so (e.g. Scottish English), but conformity to national norms is sufficient to ensure ready mutual intelligibility on a national scale. In Britain, this role is played by Received Pronunciation (RP) as codified by D. Jones, A. C. Gimson and others, and generally adopted by broadcasting authorities, dictionary makers, language course designers, etc. In its pure form, RP is the practice of a small but influential minority, but with increasing mobility and media exposure a high proportion of speakers use, either habitually or as required, a regionally-coloured approximation to RP which is universally intelligible. Regional variants differ mainly in vowel colouring. The consonant system (which has been shown to play the larger role in identifying speech) is relatively uniform and stable.

On a global scale, English is polycentric. There is no one form of English universally accepted as authoritative. Ireland, the USA, Canada and Australia have their own norms, each related to standard written English and to spoken dialectical variation in much the same way as RP. These norms are fully mutually intelligible and acceptable. All are products of the modern period and have undergone no major sound changes. There is increasingly frequent communication among the communities involved. In countries where English is not the native language, the British norm predominates in educational systems in countries which have recently become independent (India, Africa) and more generally in Europe. The General American norm predominates in the Americas and is widely used in the entertainments industry and in industrial management, in which areas it has considerable influence on British usage. Those (e.g. teachers) who have spent a considerable period in one or another English-speaking country are, of course, likely to have learned to conform to its linguistic norms. At the present time it seems reasonable in a European context to continue (as in the case of Spanish and French) to adhere to the norms of the European rather than the American variety.

By *Threshold* level, learners are able:

- as listeners, to identify the words and expressions used by native speakers of the (regionally coloured) standard variants of English (RP, Polite Scottish, Irish, General American and Australian) and by non-native speakers whose speech, though also regionally coloured, approximates to those norms;

- as speakers, to produce spoken English which is readily intelligible both to native speakers and to non-native speakers who approximate to standard norms.

Among the implications of these objectives are:

- learners should be given experience in listening to a variety of norms, and/or regionally coloured speech (including the principal non-native varieties) which approximate to those norms and remain fully intelligible;

- learners should target one of the native norms (which in a European context may well be British RP), and should approximate to it as closely as is required for full intelligibility, not only to native English speakers, but also to other non-native speakers of a comparable level.

Accordingly, learners at *Threshold* level are aware of the pronunciation in RP of the words and expressions proposed as exponents. That is to say:

- they are aware of the relation between the sound and spelling of English words, avoiding simple orthoepic errors;

- they are aware of and preserve in their own speech the vowel and, particularly, consonant contrasts of the English model they adopt;

- they are aware of and preserve in their own speech the placement of stress in polysyllabic words:

- they are able to distinguish by ear non-homophonous English words and expressions;

- they are aware of the principal meaningful contrasts in utterances carried by stress placement and intonation and will be able to recognise and understand them in the speech of others;

- they are aware of the principal respects in which the accent of learners with their mother tongue background deviates from RP in ways which are likely to impede recognition and thus communication.

The relation of *Vantage* to *Threshold* is different in respect of the phonetic aspects from what it is in other areas. There is little or no extension of content, since the speech sounds and tones of English are few in number and requisite for the realisation of functional and notional categories at *Threshold* level. Phonetic development from *Threshold* to *Vantage* is rather one of increased facility and unconscious mastery, as the articulatory and auditory skills become more thoroughly habituated.

Since Chomsky's demonstration that, contrary to the view of the behaviourists, language learning could not be reduced to processes of habit formation, it has been unfashionable to speak of habit formation in language learning at all. Yet the basic proposition, inapplicable to syntax, that control of the higher-level processes involved in the expression of thought and the conduct of conversation requires low-level phonetic and morphological processes to be automatised and pushed down out of conscious attention, remains convincing. After all, the same is true in other areas such as sport, dancing, music, etc., in which the basic physical skills are trained and then continuously refined. If, in the earliest stages of language learning, control is gained over the articulatory movements involved in producing and catenating the distinctive sounds (phonemes) of a language, then the learner should by *Threshold* have established a pronunciation and intonation which meet the above criteria as set out in Appendix A to *Threshold 1990*. The substantially increased experience gained in progressing from *Threshold* to *Vantage* will then make possible and appropriate:

- a closer approximation to the sound of the chosen model of native English speech at a sub-phonemic level;

- greater ease in catenating longer sound sequences;

- an easier and more natural use of the phonetic reduction normal in native colloquial usage including;

  - appropriate vowel reduction in unstressed syllables;
  - consonantal elision (e.g. of [t] following [s] or of [d] following [n] before another consonant as in *first thing*, the *Round Church*);

- consonantal assimilation (e.g. replacement of *t/d/n* by *p/b/m* before another bilabial consonant, or by *k, g, ng* before another velar consonant as in *goodbye, good girl*).

In words like *handbag, handgun*, and in the word *and* in relevant contexts, both the elision of the final *d* and the assimilation of *n* to *m* or *ng* are normal.

The appropriate use of phonetic reduction will make it easier for learners at *Vantage* level to establish closer and more relaxed relations with native speakers, especially in informal situations. They will, however, be aware of and take care to avoid inappropriate reduction. Fluent French speakers of English, for example, may misplace word or sentence stress and consequently reduce vowels which should be stressed and therefore not be reduced (e.g. *absolutely* for *absolutely*). This reduction further reduces their comprehensibility, as does also the voicing of voiceless consonants before another voiced consonant (e.g. the replacement of *t* by *d* in *white gloves*).

As listeners, *Vantage* learners will be able to recognise the words and sentences used by native speakers which approximate to the locally unmarked forms of the major varieties of spoken English: Southern English RP and General American, when spoken at normal conversational speed (up to about 150 words per minute). They will be able to identify the phonetic form of words they do not know, so as to be able to ask their meaning or consult a dictionary. They will be able to follow the gist either of speakers using a more highly reduced familiar register of these varieties, or of speakers of more divergent dialectal varieties (including foreign accents), though they may well need to employ compensation strategies (asking for slower and clearer repetition, seeking clarification and paraphrase, etc.) in order to understand key points.

Some form of phonetic transcription conforming to the principles of the International Phonetic Association (IPA), e.g. that used in D. Jones: *An English Pronouncing Dictionary* (14th edn. ed. A. C. Gimson) or in one of the major monolingual or bilingual dictionaries may be found useful for raising awareness and for reference purposes, but does not in itself constitute part of the *Vantage* objectives.

Intonation

The intonation of English (RP) is described in detail in such works as G. F. Arnold and J. D. O'Connor: *The Intonation of Colloquial English*. It is used by native speakers on the one hand to indicate the informational structure of sentences and on the other to express nuances of meaning, to indicate unspoken implications or reservations and to convey attitudes and emotional states. As such it plays a very important part in communication and is a frequent source of intercultural misunderstandings.

A full treatment of English intonation is beyond the scope of this book. The most important features are tone groups. Within the tone group, stressed syllables are spoken in a regular rhythm, unstressed syllables being made to fit in between the beats. The stressed syllables of words which convey lexical information (mainly nouns, adjectives, principal verbs and adverbs) are given prominence in the intonation pattern, unless the information has already been mentioned or is obvious in context. In that case, whilst continuing to mark the rhythmic beat, they are not given pitch prominence. For most practical purposes, two points of pitch prominence are of importance, the *nucleus* and the *head*. The last prominent stressed syllable in a tone group is its *nucleus*, which initiates a pitch pattern which continues to the end of the tone group, including any unstressed or stressed but non-prominent syllables that follow. The pattern used is closely related to the language function of the sentence and its grammatical category. At *Vantage* level, as at *Threshold* level, five nuclear tones should be distinguished.

1 *Low falling* This is marked by a left to right diagonal falling mark, below the line of writing, placed before the nuclear syllable [ˌ]. This mark is to be interpreted as indicating that the next syllable is stressed. Its vowel starts on a clear, low-mid tone. The voice then drops to a low creaky note and remains on this low pitch until the end of the tone group.

2 *High falling* This is similar to the low fall, except that the nuclear vowel starts on a pitch above the mid point. It is marked by placing the mark above the line of writing [ˋ].

3 *Low rising* This is marked by a rising mark placed before the nuclear syllable and below the line of writing [ˌ]. It indicates that the next syllable is stressed. Its vowel starts on a clear, low level pitch. There is then a continuous glide upward, but not rising above mid, until the end of the tone group. The glide occurs within the nuclear syllable if it is the last in the group. If it is followed by one or more non-prominent syllables (the 'tail'), stressed or unstressed, the nuclear syllable is spoken on a low level pitch and the rise spans the tail.

4 *High rising* This is shown by placing the rising mark above the line of writing [ˊ]. It indicates that the nuclear vowel starts somewhere between low and mid-level, and that the upward glide extends well above mid.

5 *Falling–rising* This may be seen as a sequence of 2 and 3. The nuclear vowel sound starts high-mid pitch and drops to a low creak. An

upward glide follows, which does not go above mid. This tone is indicated by a v-shaped mark placed before the nuclear syllable above the line of writing [˅].

Vantage learners should be familiar with the following uses of nuclear tones and be able to use them themselves as appropriate.

1 *Low falling* [ˌ] is used

   a) in declarative sentences

      i) for factual statements e.g. identifying, defining, describing and narrating as well as in answers to *wh* questions (which may be short phrases or single words);
      'This is a ˌdoor.   They 'drove to ˌLondon.   'Dogs are ˌanimals.

      ii) for expressing definite agreement or disagreement, firm denials, firm acceptance or rejection of an offer, definite statements of intention, obligation, granting or withholding permission, etc. In general, it indicates an unambiguous certainty.
      That's 'quite ˌright. You 'must ·eat your ˌdinner.

   b) in interrogative sentences answerable by *yes* or *no*

      i) in interrogation, to indicate that an answer is demanded;
      'Have you ·seen this ·man beˌfore?

      ii) in requests to indicate that they are in effect orders;
      'May I ·see your ˌdriving ·licence, ·please?
      ·Will you 'please be ˌquiet.

      iii) when a series of *yes/no* questions is posed in rapid succession;
      'Is it ˌred? 'Can you ˌeat it? 'Is it a ˌcabbage?

      iv) in tag questions, to invite agreement to a statement that is not in doubt;
      'This·tastes ˌnice, | ˌdoesn't it?

      v) in choice questions, to indicate the list of options is closed.
      'Would you prefer ˌtea | or ˌcoffee?

   c) in *wh* questions as a definite request for a piece of information
   'Where is the ˌtoilet, ·please?

   d) in imperative sentences

      i) as a direct order or prohibition;
      'Sit ˌdown.   'Don't ·smoke in ˌhere, ·please.

      ii) as an instruction;
      'Push to ·open the ˌdoor.

      iii) as a strong form of offer.
      'Have one of ˌmy ciga·rettes.

2 *High falling* [`] is used

a) in declarative sentences

i) in exclamations to indicate surprise, protest, enthusiasm, emphasis or insistence;
That's `excellent!    You are `hurting me!   'Fancy `that!

ii) to indicate contrast with an element previously mentioned or believed to be the listener's mind.
·No, it was in `Oxford that he ·studied.

b) in interrogative sentences, both those answerable by *yes* or *no* and *wh* questions

to insist on an answer being given;
'Did you `post that ·letter?

ii) to indicate surprise or irritation;
'Are you `still not ·ready?

iii) in rhetorical questions of an exclamatory type, to which no answer is sought;
'Isn't she `beautiful?

iv) in tag questions, to insist on the hearer's agreement to a proposition.
I `told you, | `didn't I?

c) in imperative sentences

i) to insist on an order or prohibition where compliance is in doubt;
`Stop it, I ·say.    'Don't `listen to him.

ii) to indicate the urgency of an instruction (e.g. because of imminent danger);
`Stop. 'Don't `move.

iii) to insist on the acceptance of an offer.
'Do let me `help you.

3 *Low rising* [ˌ] is used

a) in declarative sentences

i) (with preceding low pitches) to indicate indifference, resentment, guardedness or suspicion;
It ·doesn't ˌmatter. You ·shouldn't ·blame ˌme.

ii) (with preceding high pitch) to reassure.
There's 'no ·need to be ˌworried.

b) in interrogative questions, answerable by *yes* or *no*

    i) to ask politely for confirmation or disconfirmation (also in tag questions);
You're ˌFrench, ˌaren't you?

    ii) to make polite requests and offers;
'Would you ·please ·open the ˌwindow?
'Can I do ·anything to ˌhelp?

    iii) in choice questions, to indicate that the list is open.
'Would you like ˌtea or ˌcoffee or ·something ˌstronger?

c) in *wh* questions

    i) to indicate polite interest rather than a need for information;
'Where are you ·spending your ˌholidays?

    ii) to avoid the appearance of interrogation or peremptory questioning.
'What are you ˌdoing ·there?

d) in imperative sentences for gentle commands, especially to children, hospital patients, etc.
'Come and ·have your ·nice ˌbath.
'Just ·drink this ˌmedicine ·nicely.

4 *High rising* ['] is used

a) in declarative sentences (including isolated phrases and words used instead of full sentences)

    i) to convert a statement into a question;
You were ·born in 'Scotland?

    ii) to query what someone has said.
You ·say you're 'thirsty?

b) in interrogative questions answerable by *yes* or *no*

    i) (with preceding low pitch) to indicate a casual enquiry;
(Would you) ·care for a 'sandwich?

    ii) to repeat a question (with change of 1st and 2nd person) before answering.
A 'sandwich? Would I ·care for a 'sandwich?

c) in *wh* questions

    i) to repeat a question (with change of 1st and 2nd person) before answering;
(in answer to 'Where do you ˌlive?) ·Where do I 'live?

ii) (with the *wh* word as nucleus) to ask for repetition of information given but not heard (or not understood). (querying He ·lives in [unintelligible].) He ·lives 'where? 'Where does he ·live?

d) in imperative sentences to repeat an order, instruction or offer while deciding whether or how to comply (replying to 'Sit˰ down, please)   'Sit 'down? 'Why ˎnot?

5 *Falling-rising* [˅] is used

a) in declarative sentences to convey various implications

i) warnings;
That ·jug is ˅hot!

ii) corrections;
Her ·dress 'isn't ˅blue, | it's ˅green.

iii) demurral and limited agreement (with implied disagreement on the major issue);
I 'don't ·know if I a ·gree with ˅that.
˅Yes, | he 'is an ˅active ·person.

iv) mental reservations in making promises;
˅Yes, | I ˅will be ·good. At ·least, I'll ˅try.

v) uncertainty and hesitation;
Yes ˅possibly. | I 'can't be ˅certain.

vi) to soften the effect of bad news, conflict of views, etc.;
You 'haven't ·done very ˅well, I'm a ·fraid.
You're ˅wrong, you ·know.

vii) (with attached tag questions) anxious query;
You 'do ˅love me, ·don't you?

viii) discouragement of a possible course of action;
You can 'go to the ·cinema if you ˅like.

ix) tentative advice;
If 'I were ˅you, | I'd ˎthink a ·bout it.

x) implying that something has been left unsaid, which contrasts with, or contradicts what has been overtly stated;
Your o ·pinion is ˅interesting. (**implying**: but I 'don't a ˎgree.)

xi) to query what has been said, implying that it is mistaken or untrue.
'Seven ·eights are ·fifty ˅four?

b) in interrogative questions answered by *yes* or *no*

    i) to add a note of warning or doubt;
       Are you ^ˇsure you ·locked the ·door?

    ii) when the expected answer to the question may be
        unwelcome to the person giving it.
       'Have you ·thought what might ·happen if you ^ˇdid?

c) in *wh* questions

    i) to repeat a question, focusing on the key issue in contrast
       with other possible issues;
       'What did I· do on ^ˇFriday of ·last ·week?

    ii) (with the *wh* word as nucleus) to query a statement, implying
        scepticism regarding the element queried by the *wh* word
        employed.
       ^ˇWhere did he ·find your ·purse?

d) in imperative sentences

    i) for issuing warnings rather than commands or instructions;
       'Watch where you're ^ˇgoing.
       'Don't ·try to ^ˇpull the ·door ·open.

    ii) (with the imperative as nucleus) for pleading.
       ^ˇDo ·try to be ·little more ·careful.

Every tone group contains a *nucleus*. Many short utterances will comprise a single tone group, containing only one prominent syllable, which is then the nucleus of the tone group. Where there is more than one prominent syllable, the last of these is the nucleus and the first is the *head*. The head is usually marked by a jump up in pitch to a high-mid level. The actual pitch varies from mid to high, depending on the attitude of the speaker towards what he or she is saying and towards the hearer. The higher the level, the more cheerful and friendly the speaker sounds. The (high) head is marked in the texts by an upright line before the syllable concerned, above the line of writing ['].

Non-prominent syllables, stressed or unstressed, which precede the head, are spoken on a low mid pitch. Those following a high head are kept on the same level, or form a descending sequence. Those following the nucleus conform to the configuration of the nucleus, as elaborated above. Stressed non-prominent syllables are marked in texts by a dot raised to mid-letter height [·]. As stated, they mark rhythmic beats in the utterance, but have no effect on the pitch pattern. Non-prominent unstressed syllables are left unmarked.

Many, perhaps most, short exchanges in conversation consist of single tone groups. Longer utterances may simply juxtapose tone groups as already described. However, compound (**and, but, either, or**) and complex (**if, because, when**) sentences may have two or more closely linked tone groups. Only in the last of these has the nucleus the functions listed above. The sequence is then termed a *major tone group*, and its completion is shown in a text with the mark [|||]. The constituent *minor tone groups* are marked [||]. The following are the most common types of sequence, and should be within the productive and receptive competence of *Vantage* learners:

1 Unemphatic, non-contrastive sentences

non-final group	final group
low rising	low falling
'When you ·see ˌJohn |	'tell him to ˌphone me. ||

2 Contrastive sentences

non-final group	final group
falling-rising	high falling
But 'when you see ˅Harry |	'tell him I've ·left the ˋcountry.||

3 Main statement and modifier (non-contrastive)

low falling	low rising
I'm 'leaving for ˌGermany |	on ˌFriday.||

4 Main statement and supplement

low fall	low fall
He ·lives in ˌLondon |	in a 'semi-de ·tached ·house in ˌPeckham.||

5 In all cases of apposition, the same nuclear tone is used for both tone groups. The word **too** similarly repeats the tone of its antecedent nucleus

'John ˌSmith, \| a com ˌputer ·programmer \| ·lives in ˌCambridge, \| a uniˌversity ·city.\|\|
His ˌbrother ·lives there, \| ˌtoo.\|\|

Note In this book, [|||] is normally omitted at the end of examples consisting of a single sentence.

Learners at *Vantage* level will have progressed well beyond the stage regarded as adequate at *Threshold* level, where learners are expected to recognise and understand only the most common intonation patterns used in RP and to employ rising and falling nuclei appropriately in their own speech, organising the phrasing, stressing and rhythm of tone groups in accordance with RP norms. *Vantage* learners will have receptive and productive command of word stress, i.e. they will know which syllables carry primary and secondary stress, or are unstressed. In the case of words carrying double stress, they can recognise the word concerned despite the shifting of main stress following the principle of rhythmical variation (e.g. *She is just six**teen**, having just had her **six**teenth birthday*). In connected speech, they will observe the regular 'beat' of stressed syllables, adjusting the length of syllables accordingly. They will be able to group words appropriately into sense groups and also to recognise and interpret as well as produce intonation patterns routinely in accordance with the principles set out above. For this reason, the intonation of example sentences is not marked in Chapter 5–7 or Appendix A of *Vantage*, unless the use of a particular intonation is specified as part of the exponent of a functional category.